# THE CROSS
# HE BORE

# THE CROSS
# HE BORE

Meditations on the
Sufferings of the
Redeemer

Frederick S. Leahy

THE BANNER OF TRUTH TRUST

# THE BANNER OF TRUTH TRUST

3 Murrayfield Road, Edinburgh EH12 6EL, UK
P.O. Box 621, Carlisle, PA 17013, USA

\*

First published 1996
Reprinted 2007
Reprinted 2011
Reprinted 2015

© Mrs Margaret Leahy 2007

ISBN:
Print: 978 0 85151 693 6
EPUB: 978 1 84871 539 4
Kindle: 978 1 84871 540 0

\*

Typeset in 10.5/13.5 pt Sabon at
the Banner of Truth Trust

Printed in the USA by
Versa Press, Inc.,
East Peoria, IL

TO MY STUDENTS –
They have kept the faith
and made it known

# Contents

# Foreword

'All the wisdom of believers', wrote Calvin, 'is comprehended in the cross of Christ.' It is thus a particular pleasure to commend this series of meditations, from a former colleague on the faculty of the Reformed Theological College, on the sufferings of the Saviour. This volume is excellent throughout, yet it seems to have three especially significant virtues.

It provides us with solid *instruction*. In addition to more than thirty years teaching systematic theology, Frederick S. Leahy spent a lifetime in the ministry of the Word. In these pages, preacher, pastor and theologian come together in a happy unity. No words are wasted. There is nothing of the frothy and insubstantial. Here is satisfying truth, painstakingly quarried and crafted for the needs of God's people. A judicious selection of gems from the writings of others provides further enrichment and stimulus to thought.

This is a work which gives full play to a disciplined and sanctified *imagination*. Some of his past students may be surprised at such a choice of words, since Professor Leahy's adamant rejection of speculation in the formulation of doctrine has become legendary. Yet the Bible is more than a catalogue of abstract propositions and the task of the preacher is surely to mediate the truth through all the powers of his renewed personality. D. Martyn Lloyd-Jones was right to complain that 'we have all become so scientific that there is but little room left for imagination. This, to me, is most regrettable because imagination in preaching is most important and most helpful . . . what it does is make the Truth lively and living'.

Lastly, these studies recall us to the neglected art of *meditation*. We are too apt to hurry past the cross, to undervalue, in spite of ourselves, the supreme mystery of the ages by a shallow assumption that we know it all. We don't and never will. But we need to take time to learn as much as we can. We need to 'behold', to 'survey', to 'stand and stare'. In rereading these chapters, I found myself more than once compelled by emotion to stop – and then to worship. I cannot help feeling that this is exactly how they were written and that the author's chief desire is that each of us who reads should be brought to gaze in fresh understanding and gratitude upon 'the Son of God, who loved me and gave himself for me'.

EDWARD DONNELLY

Principal,
Reformed Theological College,
Belfast,
Northern Ireland

# Introduction

During my student days in Edinburgh, I happened to be on my way through Glasgow and finding that I had time on my hands stopped at a well-known Christian bookshop to browse. There I discovered Dr Klaas Schilder's trilogy on the sufferings of Christ. It had just been translated into English. I bought this for the sum of 17/6 (85 p) per volume – reckless expenditure for a divinity student in the late forties, and probably deserving rebuke. However that purchase proved to be an investment, and over the years I have turned to those volumes again and again, and have been immensely helped by Schilder's insights. There are echoes of Schilder in the following chapters and I wish to record my indebtedness to him. During the same period my revered mentor, Professor R. A. Finlayson, was showing me aspects of Christ's redemptive sufferings which previously I had not considered.

As the cross is central in God's eternal decrees, and in the actual redemption of his people, so it should be central in the thinking and experience of the individual Christian. It is my conviction, and at times my sad experience, that as the cross goes out of focus in the Christian's life, coldness and backsliding set in.

It is not my intention in these brief chapters to give a detailed account of the trial and crucifixion of our Lord. That is done in the Gospels infinitely better than by any mere man or woman. Rather, I have selected certain passages which help us to meditate on what the Saviour endured for our salvation. If our meditation on the cross be meagre, can our love for the Saviour be great?

Much of the material in this book is based on a series of short articles that appeared in 1991 in *The Covenanter Witness*, the magazine of the Reformed Presbyterian Church. Except where otherwise stated, the translation of Scripture employed is that of the English Standard Version.

F. S. L.

1996

# I

# MAN OF SORROWS

Then Jesus went with them to a place called Gethsemane . . . And . . . he began to be sorrowful and
troubled (*Matt.* 26:36, 37).

T he record of our Lord's passion looms large in the
Gospels. Almost one third of the space is devoted to
the account of his sufferings. The Gospels are not mere
biographies; indeed, strictly speaking, they are not biographies at all, for they are silent on much of the earthly
life of Christ. Their purpose is theological, to convey to
mankind what God has done in Christ for the salvation
of sinners. They proclaim good news and the cross is the
centre of that saving message. While they speak of the
joy and the peace of Christ, the emphasis is on his suffering. He is presented essentially as the man of sorrows.
Matthew, in his account of the agony in Gethsemane,
brings that fact into sharp focus.

## AFTER THE FEAST

The statement in Matthew 26:36, 37 is significant. Christ
has known sorrow before this, but the assertion that
in Gethsemane he *began* to be sorrowful and troubled

indicates a sudden steep descent into the billows of distress. Now, as never before, all God's waves and billows began to sweep over him (*Psa.* 42:7). What a contrast to the sweet calm and peace of the upper room! He and his disciples had just sung from that wondrous Passover hymn, the Hallel (*Psalms* 113–118) and Christ sang that hymn as it had never·been sung before and as it never could be sung again, for he was about to fulfil it as he went to his cross.

Now the singing has stopped. The holy peace is no more and an awful anguish suddenly grips the soul of the Redeemer as he *begins* to be 'sore amazed, and to be very heavy' (*Mark* 14:33, KJV; Moffatt translates, 'appalled and agitated'). Referring to the expression 'sore amazed', Dr Frederick Krummacher says that Mark 'makes use of a word in the original which implies a sudden and horrifying alarm at a terrific object . . . something approached Him which threatened to rend His nerves, and the sight of it to freeze the blood in His veins'. The feast is over. The sacrifice it symbolized is imminent. The language used in the original is vivid and forceful. It indicates torment of soul, a state of intense anguish. 'My soul', he said, 'is very sorrowful even to death.' This is no ordinary distress. No man had ever experienced such distress before and no one would ever do so again. In a unique sense Jesus of Nazareth was a 'man of sorrows'. His acquaintance with grief was unparalleled.

After the feast Christ was suddenly plunged into an abyss of anguish so intense that he declared himself overwhelmed to the point of death. Calvin says, 'Though

God had already tried his Son by certain preparatory exercises, he now wounds him more sharply by a nearer prospect of death and strikes his mind with a terror to which he had not been accustomed.'

## FACING DEATH

It has been common to contrast the calm and serene death of Socrates, condemned to drink the poisoned cup, with the agony of Christ at the prospect of death. Socrates faced death fearlessly and stoically because he had mastered the art of suppressing his emotions, but in this, as Klaas Schilder reminds us, he lived only a half-life and died only a half-death. Christ, on the contrary, suppressed nothing either in life or in death, and in the cold shadows of Gethsemane he gave full vent to his feelings, full rein to his emotions. Indeed, he brought men to witness (however briefly) his agony and, by his Spirit, had a detailed account of his sufferings recorded.

It is not necessary to turn to Socrates in order to contrast calmness in the hour of death with the dread that gripped the Saviour's soul. Countless numbers of Christ's own redeemed people have faced torture and martyrdom with courage and serenity. They were more than conquerors, facing their ordeal with praise on their lips. Like Stephen they saw the glory of God as they stepped into eternity. But the death of Christ is different from every other death. True, the physical aspect of his death has much in common with other deaths, but there the comparison ends. He died as the Surety for his people and as their Substitute. Not only must he experience physical death, but also he must taste eternal death – damnation – separation from God! In all of this he must grapple with Satan and destroy death itself (*Gen.* 3:15, *I Cor.* 15:26). There is no analogy between the death of Socrates and that of Christ. Christ's death is not to be compared with any other. True, but why the 'loud cries and tears' (*Heb.* 5:7), the mental distress, the nameless grief?

## ENTERING THE DARKNESS

It is true that Christ in his sinless human nature recoiled from the prospect of death and shrank from it with horror, for death came with sin. It is also true that he sensed the approach of Satan who after the temptation in the wilderness 'departed from him until an opportune time' (*Luke* 4:13). It is also the case that he anticipated the approaching wrath of a holy God. But none of these facts can account for the distress and sorrow that were to prove too much for unaided human nature (albeit sinless) to bear. There must be something deeper and *more actual* to account for our Lord's struggle in Gethsemane.

Gethsemane means 'the oil press'. David could say, 'I am like a green olive tree in the house of God' (*Psa.* 52:8). Israel in her long history could say the same. But the suffering Saviour could say it best of all, for there in Gethsemane – the oil press – he was crushed and bruised without mercy. But *how* and *why*? How is the sudden and dramatic change of atmosphere between the upper room and Gethsemane to be explained, even in a measure? Christ knew all along the death that awaited him. He had grappled with Satan and his legions more than once.

He had repeatedly spoken of his death to his disciples, telling them what that death would accomplish. He had prayed with the utmost confidence in his high priestly prayer (*John* 17). Why, then, is there this sudden plunge into such awful agony, why this shuddering horror? Why is *this* fruit of the olive tree so severely crushed? Why does the divine record say that in Gethsemane our Lord BEGAN to be sorrowful, sorrowful in a new and terrible way? Was it not because *God began forsaking him then*? How else is this sorrow unto death to be understood?

'Jesus wept', but never like this. No previous sorrow of his could match this. At the time of his arrest he declared, 'Shall I not drink the cup which the Father *has given me*?' (*John* 18:11). That cup was constantly in view as he prayed in Gethsemane. What cup? 'THIS CUP' – not some future cup. The cup that was *symbolized* in the feast (*Matt.* 26:27,28) was now *actual*: God was placing it in the Saviour's hands and it carried the stench of hell. But stop!

Schilder is right. 'Gethsemane is not a field of study for our intellect. It is a sanctuary of our faith'. Lord, forgive us for the times we have read about Gethsemane with dry eyes.

## 2

# PRAYERFUL SUBMISSION

'My Father, if it be possible, let this cup pass from me; nevertheless not as I will, but as you will' (*Matt.* 26:39).

The agony of our Lord in the garden was a once-for-all event. There is nothing in human experience that is remotely like it. It is bordering on blasphemy to speak of someone's Gethsemane or Calvary. The 'hour' of Christ's passion is high noon in the day of human history. We are now living in the afternoon. As Schilder puts it neatly, 'The clock can strike twelve only once in a single day. Therefore the clock of Gethsemane can strike only once in the world'.

The account of Christ's sorrows in Gethsemane is to be read with wonder and awe, not to be dissected or psychoanalysed – nor indeed can it be. In Gethsemane there was, as R. A. Finlayson says, 'something transacted that brings us completely out of our depth, yet something that has such a distinct bearing on our redemption that we dare not pass it by'.

### THE AGONIZING ENTREATY

The cup placed in Christ's hands by the Father induced a heaviness and dread he had not previously known and his sinless humanity shrank back from the horror of that cup. In the Old Testament the term 'cup' frequently refers to God's punishment of sin. 'Let him rain coals on the wicked; fire and sulphur and a scorching wind shall be the portion of their cup' (*Psa.* 11:6). 'Wake yourself, wake yourself, stand up, O Jerusalem, you who have drunk from the hand of the LORD the cup of his wrath, who have drunk to the dregs the bowl, the cup of staggering' (*Isa.* 51:17). J. A. Motyer who translates, 'the goblet of the cup of trembling', a double emphasis, sees in this verse 'a picture of being hopelessly, irretrievably under the wrath of God'. The Saviour knew his Old Testament and now he was profoundly aware of the nature of the cup that he had been given and so he prayed with the utmost intensity, that, *if possible*, it might *pass from him*. Agonizingly he entreated the Father, first on his knees and then prostrate on the ground, that this awful cup be removed. As we read the biblical account, we hear the cry of his wounded spirit. Is there no other way? No way consonant with the Father's redemptive purpose, the mission entrusted to him from all eternity? Is there no other way consistent with righteousness and God's glory? Is the cross the only way?

How clearly the true humanity of Christ is seen in Gethsemane, more so than in much of our standard dogmatics! For evangelicals are so concerned to defend the deity of Christ, and rightly so, that often they hardly know how to handle his humanity! Here, in Gethsemane, we see the sinless, finite humanity of Christ in deep and terrible distress. Calvin said that Christ had horror at the prospect of death because 'he had before his eyes the dreadful tribunal of God, and the judge himself armed with inconceivable vengeance; and because of our sins, the load of which was laid upon him, pressed him down with their enormous weight. There is no reason to wonder, therefore, if the dreadful abyss of destruction tormented him grievously with fear and anguish.' Yes, fear and anguish; but, unlike the experience of all others, it was fear untainted by sin. It was Ambrose who said, 'He grieved for me, who had no cause of grief for himself; and, laying aside the delights of the eternal Godhead, he experiences the affliction of my weakness.'

## THE AWFUL SILENCE

Again and again the Saviour casts himself on the Father's bosom in earnest supplication, but there is no answer to his anguished cry. Heaven remains silent. He rises and falls, rises and falls, but it seems almost as if God were thrusting him away. For the moment the door of his Father's house remains fast closed, despite his repeated knocking. No Father meets him with outstretched arms! And so he learns that there is no other way.

'The cup of horror', writes Krummacher, 'does not pass from the trembling sufferer; on the contrary, its contents become every moment more bitter. Louder sound the complaints of the agonizing Saviour; more urgent becomes his prayer; but the Lofty One is silent, and heaven seems barred with a thousand bolts.' He complains in the sense of expressing grief and pain, not in the secondary sense of murmuring.

For Christ to be our Saviour there was no other way than the way of the cross. God's righteousness demanded it, our sin required it and Satan feared it. And for those who would be saved from sin and its consequences, there is no other way than the way of that cross where God's holy conscience has been satisfied, sin has been dealt with and Satan has been routed.

Thus it was that amid 'loud cries and tears' our Lord 'learned obedience through what he suffered' (*Heb.* 5:7, 8). That is, as the incarnate Son, who fully shares our humanity, he learned the *cost* of obedience. He never needed correction. Now he learned what it meant to be obedient to the death of the cross. Consequently the Apostle Paul could write, 'For as by the one man's disobedience the many were made sinners, so by the one man's obedience the many will be made righteous' (*Rom.* 5:19).

Was the Father indifferent to the Son's passionate pleadings in Gethsemane? Did he ever for a moment cease to be well pleased with him? Far from it. The writer to the Hebrews assures us that the Saviour 'was heard because of his reverence' (5:7). The proof of his being heard is his resurrection from the dead. In that sense he was 'saved from death'.

## THE UNWAVERING OBEDIENCE

Never for a moment did Christ falter in his obedience. Never did he cease to love his Father. Never did he cease to trust his Father. Never did he doubt his Father's justice. Love and justice are in perfect balance in Gethsemane. There could be no turning away from the commission his Father had given him. Therefore his obedience was total and unwavering. That is evident from his very presence in Gethsemane. He went there voluntarily. All along his sole desire was that his Father's will might be done. Indeed he prayed that his own will might *not be done*. He concluded, 'My Father, if this cannot pass unless I drink it, your will be done' (*Matt.* 26:42). His desires and his Father's are really one: there is no disharmony in Gethsemane, no clash of wills. Undoubtedly there is keen awareness of divine wrath and yet there is total trust in God; but these ingredients, as George Smeaton remarks, 'though they are distinct, are by no means incompatible. The one was due to His office as the sin-bearer; the other was expressive of His personal relation.'

In Gethsemane it was never a question whether the Saviour would obey or disobey. In Eden God asked, 'Adam, where are you?' In a sense the question was repeated in Gethsemane and this Adam did not try to hide; he had no need to; his whole response was clearly, 'Here am I!' Willingly and voluntarily the good shepherd laid down his life for the sheep. As that eminent 19th-century theologian, William Symington, points out

Vicarious satisfaction can never be compulsory; voluntariness enters into its very essence.

And so Matthew Henry can say, 'He grounds his own willingness upon the Father's will, and resolves the matter wholly into that.'

Because the suffering of the Redeemer was in his human nature, there never was and never could be any rupture within the depths of the divine being. Nor was there ever a moment of doubt or reluctance in Christ's experience. When, at times, Reformed theologians speak of Christ experiencing near despair, despondency, not always being assured of victory and see him as 'a broken man', they do so rashly and without the slightest biblical warrant. Even when Christ for a time lost the sense of his Father's presence and affection, he continued to know him solely by faith: he is 'the founder and perfecter of our faith' (*Heb.* 12:2).

As we meditate on Christ's prayerful submission in Gethsemane, we should realise that there, as Philip E. Hughes puts it, 'we see him enduring our hell so that we might be set free to enter his heaven'. And so at unspeakable cost he drank 'the cup' to the very last drop. 'Shall I not drink the cup that the Father has given me?' (*John* 18:11). What obedience! What love! What mystery!

> But none of the ransomed ever knew
> How deep were the waters cross'd;
> Nor how dark was the night
> That the Lord pass'd through . . .

Now he gives to his people 'the cup of salvation' (*Psa.* 116:13). These two cups, one so bitter, the other so sweet, stand side by side: the one cup necessitated the other. One cup was emptied that the other might be filled to overflowing. The first cup guaranteed the second. Both cups are precious and bear the hallmark of sovereign grace. 'What shall I render to the LORD for all his benefits to me? I will lift up the cup of salvation and call on the name of the LORD (*Psa.* 116:12, 13).

3

# STRENGTHENED TO SUFFER

And there appeared to him an angel from heaven, strengthening him (*Luke* 22:43).

Without the inspired record of the Redeemer's agony in Gethsemane, we would have a much less vivid impression of the peculiar intensity of his griefs and the crushing weight of the load that he bore. As Dr Campbell Morgan remarks, 'All I can say is that as I ponder [Gethsemane], through that darkened window, there is a mystic light shining, showing me the terrors of the Cross more clearly than I see them even when I come to Calvary.' Gethsemane is not a place for hurried theological tourism: it is where the believer must linger, watch and pray.

## THE SELF-DENIAL

Our Lord's life of perfect obedience as the Suffering Servant, culminating in the agony of Gethsemane and Golgotha, was characterized throughout by self-renunciation. 'He made himself of no reputation' (*Phil.* 2:7, KJV). This is commonly translated to read that Christ 'emptied himself', and B. B. Warfield regards this as a mistranslation. Certainly Christ could not have emptied himself of his divine essence, for then he would have ceased to be God. The kenotic theory, that Christ divested himself of his deity, or at least of certain divine attributes, became popular with 19th-century German theologians and survived in various modified forms. It presents a Jesus who is either 'shrunken deity' or else not truly human. And as Warfield says cogently, 'No Christian heart will be satisfied with a Christ in whom there was no Godhead at all while He was on earth, and in whom there may be no manhood at all now that He has gone to heaven'. Warfield stresses that there is no half-way house between the doctrine that Christ is both God and man and that Christ is merely man. Someone has said that a Jesus who is just less than God is like a bridge broken at the farther end. Such a Jesus could not deliver from Satan and sin, and such a Jesus the Bible does not present.

The acceptance of 'the form of a servant (or slave)' by the eternal Son of God and his 'being born in the likeness of men' describes the 'kenosis', the self-renunciation of Christ. Scripture takes us no further than that, but it does show us Christ as the suffering servant, submissive to his Father's will and following a course of active self-denial. In that sense he could say, 'The Father is greater than I' (*John* 14:28). The reference is clearly to his incarnate state, not his essential being, and must not be understood in such a way as to conflict with his other statement, 'I and the Father are one' (*John* 10:30). Christ's self-restraint as servant is obvious and impressive. 'When he suffered, he made no threats. Instead, he entrusted himself to him who judges justly' (*1 Pet.* 2:23, NIV).

This same self-restraint of Christ was evident at the time of his arrest, when he asked, 'Do you think that I cannot appeal to my Father, and he will at once send me more than twelve legions of angels? But how then should the Scriptures be fulfilled, that it must be so?' (*Matt.* 26:53,54). It is noteworthy, in this connection, that when, in response to the soldier's affirmation that they sought Jesus of Nazareth, he replied 'I AM', they 'drew back and fell to the ground' (*John* 18:6). Calvin says, 'There was no want of power in him, therefore, to restrain their hands if he had thought proper, but he wished to obey his Father, by whose decree he knew that he was called to die.' And Calvin adds, 'We may infer from this how dreadful and alarming to the wicked the voice of Christ will be, when he shall ascend his throne to judge the world.' Christ's whole earthly life, however, was one of humble obedience. He 'did not please himself' (*Rom.* 15:3). Professor John Murray comments, 'He did not by flinching evade any of the stroke.'

## THE COVENANT BOND

While our Lord in Gethsemane received no answer to his repeated knocking on heaven's door, he knew, from that profound silence, that he must drink the awful chalice that the Father had placed in his hands. Always he was fully aware of the covenant bond between the Father, representing the Trinity, and himself, representing his people – the covenant of grace. Again and again he addressed the Father, a word so often on his lips, as 'my Father' and 'my God'. That is covenant language.

Christ knew that the Father smote him for the salvation of his people. Before going to Gethsemane, he warned his disciples that they would soon forsake him, quoting from Zechariah, 'I will strike the shepherd, and the sheep of the flock will be scattered' (*Matt.* 26:31). He willingly submitted to the rod. In Gethsemane he virtually said, 'Here am I.' His obedience was covenant obedience. He was ever mindful of his eternal undertaking as the Surety and Mediator of his people, a thought that is dominant in his high priestly prayer (*John* 17). He never doubted that holy decree by which he came into the world to save sinners. And so the darker the night, the greater the storm and fiercer the conflict, the more he reached out to his Father and rested in his sovereign will.

## THE OUTSTRETCHED HAND

Although the entreaties of Christ in the garden met with oppressive silence, it does not follow that the Father was indifferent to the Son's anguish or that his prayer was unheeded. Christ's sufferings were an essential part of his satisfaction of divine justice, and the Father was actively involved even when he deprived the Son of the sense of his presence. Finlayson puts it movingly when he says that 'the finger of the Father was upon the pulse of the lonely Sufferer in Gethsemane, and when the heart-beats of the One in conflict seemed to weaken, Heaven concerned itself about Him, and an angel was commissioned to hasten to His physical aid'. There was an outstretched hand, his Father's hand – even in the darkness – and Christ knew it. Initially the presence of the angel must have brought some modicum of comfort to the Sufferer. It came at a moment when unaided human nature could no longer take the strain. It was a critical moment. Christ knew that his sorrow was 'unto death' (*Matt.* 26:38, KJV), and as Dr Frederick Godet remarks, this was 'no figure of rhetoric'. But it was not the Father's will that the Saviour should die in the garden, and just as after the temptation in the wilderness angels ministered to him (*Matt.* 4:11, *Mark* 1:13), so now he was strengthened by an angel. How strange is the sight! A creature sent to minister to the Creator! But then, as man he 'for a little while was made lower than the angels' (*Heb.* 2:9). Here the theologians run out of answers. Mercifully so! There is a place for mystery. There is need for ground on which, in a unique sense, one walks by faith and not by sight. Bishop Ryle well says of Christ's experience in Gethsemane, 'It is a depth which we have no line to fathom.'

For one fleeting moment immense joy must have leaped within Christ's soul as the Father's hand touched him. This was a message from home. Heaven was behind him. He was forsaken, but not disowned. His Father was there, somewhere in the darkness. His loud cries and tears had not been unnoticed.

## THE AGGRAVATED CONDITION

Whatever comfort the angel brought the Saviour was transient. The angel's mission was not to bring relief to Christ, but to strengthen him for further and even greater anguish – anguish quite beyond human endurance. It was then that our Lord 'being in an agony . . . prayed more earnestly; and his sweat became like great drops of blood falling down to the ground' (*Luke* 22:44). The angel's presence served to aggravate his suffering. It was in order that the suffering might not only be maintained, but also that it might be intensified that the angel was sent. The battle must go on. It was too soon to say 'Finished'. The lamb of God must have the strength of a lion in this struggle.

Luke the physician gives a most graphic account of Christ's agony, and as Dr William Hobart of Trinity College, Dublin, pointed out in his fascinating study 'The Medical Language of St Luke' (first published in 1882), the terms used by Luke, translated in the KJV 'strengthen', 'agony', 'sweat', 'drops of blood', are all medical terms. For example, the term translated 'drops of blood', was currently used in medical circles for a 'clot of coagulated blood', and from it comes the English word 'thrombosis'. So Moffatt translates, 'His sweat dropping to the ground like clots of blood'. Luke had a special interest in and was granted a unique insight into this agony of our Lord, whose manhood was thus reinforced to endure an otherwise crushing load. This awful sweat was all the more remarkable in that it happened on a night so cold that even the soldiers in the high priest's courtyard found it necessary to light a fire to warm themselves.

No wonder the godly 'Rabbi' Duncan expressed the hope that if he arrived in heaven (there was always an 'if' with this outstanding saint of God) 'first I shall look for the face of my Lord, and then I shall enquire for the angel that came to help my Lord in the hour of his agony in Gethsemane'. That should be the sentiment of every Christian who in thought and experience visits this hallowed spot.

> Death and the curse were in our cup.
> O Christ, 'twas full for Thee!
> But Thou hast drained the last dark drop,
> 'Tis empty now for me.
> That bitter cup, love drank it up,
> Now blessing's draught for me.

This is well stated in the Reformed (Dutch) form of the holy supper: He 'took the curse upon Himself in order that He might satisfy us with His blessing'. That is fundamental. It is true that Christ preached the gospel, but as R. W. Dale says so well, 'The real truth is that while He came to preach the Gospel, His chief object in coming was that there might be a Gospel to preach.'

# 4

# SATAN'S HOUR

'This is your hour, and the power of darkness' (*Luke* 22:53).

As we reflect on Christ's agony in Gethsemane, it becomes apparent that just as Adam's disobedience in a garden brought ruin upon mankind, so the obedience of 'the last Adam' in this garden was essential for man's salvation. As C. H. Spurgeon says, 'Gethsemane supplies the medicine for the ills which followed upon the forbidden fruit of Eden.' When the Saviour, having eaten the Passover and instituted the holy supper, went across the brook Kedron to Gethsemane, not only was he going to a spot where he loved to go for prayer and rest, but also to a place where his enemies could easily find him. John tells us, 'Judas . . . also knew the place' (18:2).

When the hour approached for Christ to be betrayed, he deliberately went to his favourite haunt, well known to the traitor. J. J. Van Oosterzee speaks of 'the firm control with which He avoids every word and deed which could tend to His liberation'. Christ met his captors at the entrance of the garden. How easily he could have escaped arrest! But in the spirit of voluntary self-surrender he met his enemies. It was here that Judas, in the company of soldiers, gave the prearranged signal whereby they might identify the Nazarene – an ostentatious kiss of apparent affection. It was an act of black treason.

*This was the most unkindest cut of all . . .*

That kiss was a stab in the heart, a dastardly act of disloyalty on the part of one who had been treated as a trusted friend.

> Yea, ev'n mine own familiar friend,
>     on whom I did rely,
> Who ate my bread, ev'n he his heel
>     against me lifted high.
> (*Psa.* 41:9, *Scottish Metrical Version*)

'I am not speaking of all of you', said Christ, 'I know whom I have chosen. But the Scripture will be fulfilled, "He who ate my bread has lifted his heel against me"' (*John* 13:18). Commenting on this Bishop Horne remarks, 'The sufferings of the church, like those of her Redeemer, generally begin at home; her open enemies can do her no harm, until her pretended friends have delivered her into their hands . . .'

The 'son of perdition' had done what he had to do and the soldiers arrested and bound the One who stood so calmly in their midst. Christ's hands were firmly bound, but not before they had once again been stretched out in mercy as he healed Malchus' ear (*Luke* 22:51). Amy Carmichael says, 'The last thing the Lord Jesus did before His hands were bound was to heal'. It was at the moment of his arrest that the Saviour made the profound statement, 'This is your hour, and the power of darkness'.

## A PREDETERMINED HOUR

The hour of Christ's arrest, trial and crucifixion was determined in the counsels of the Godhead from all eternity. Although slain by 'wicked hands', Christ's suffering and death were 'according to the definite plan and foreknowledge of God' (*Acts* 2:23). This hour was predestined, and because predestined it was prophesied: prophecy depends on predestination. Thus both Matthew and Mark, in their account of Christ's arrest, quote his saying, 'All this has taken place, that the Scriptures of the prophets might be fulfilled' (*Matt.* 26:56). Clearly, Christ saw his captivity in terms of God's sovereign schedule. All of history had moved unerringly and inexorably to this hour. Schilder states this so well:

> God has arranged all of the preceding centuries, all of the intervolutions of time, all of the events from Genesis 1:1 up to this moment – has arranged and moulded them, has had them converge in such a way that there would be a place for this hour, the hour in which His Son will be bound . . . He allowed neither the forces above nor the forces below to tamper with the clock of history. He directed the battles of Caesars, the conflicts of kings, the migration of peoples, the world wars, the courses of stars and sun and moon, the change of epochs, and the complex movements of all things in the world in such a way that this hour would come and had to come.

Those who see the expression 'the power of darkness' as merely referring to the fact that darkness provides a welcome cover for crime and that Satan motivates men to evil deeds at such a time miss the point here. Christ was conscious of intense satanic activity. Here Moffatt's translation brings out the meaning: 'This is your hour, and the dark Power has its way.'

This statement of the Saviour attributing his arrest to 'the power of darkness' shows that *initially* the plans of his enemies would succeed, not just because they came to him under cover of darkness, but essentially because in this hour Satan and his forces were permitted by God to subject Christ to further suffering and humiliation. God *reserved* this hour for Satan. In all of time this hour was especially his. The darkness of which Christ spoke was the darkness of evil and of the prince of darkness. In this dread hour Satan had free rein. In the case of Job God set a limit to Satan's activity. In the experience of Christ there were no limits to Satan's onslaught. He was free to do his worst, and he did.

Gethsemane and Calvary marked high noon in the world's long day, and God's permission was absolute as Satan mustered his legions for the decisive encounter. The first Adam had been easy prey. How would he fare with this Adam? As Satan entered the battlefield he did so fully conscious of the Word of God: 'He shall bruise your head, and you shall bruise his heel'. Did he recall his cynical contempt for God's Word earlier when he asked, 'Did God actually say . . . ?' (*Gen.* 3:1). Or did he fear the sentence passed in Eden? Doubtless he did. But the hour was fixed. It was decreed by God. When tempting Christ in the wilderness, Satan had done his utmost to deflect him from this hour, to take some other road than the way of the cross, but all in vain. Now the battle had commenced in earnest. Nothing could stop it. *This is your hour, Satan!*

## CHRIST'S HOUR

Because God sovereignly chose this hour, there is a sense in which it must also be seen as Christ's hour, the hour appointed for his sacrifice. Thus it is called Satan's hour in one place and Christ's in another. There is no contradiction in this. The same event is viewed from different angles.

Throughout his earthly ministry Christ was conscious of an hour which would be peculiarly his as well as peculiarly Satan's. This aspect of his Messianic consciousness receives prominence in John's Gospel. Repeatedly the Lord declares, 'My time is not yet come'. When, on one occasion, the Jews tried to arrest him, they were unable to do so: 'No one laid a hand on him, *because his hour had not yet come*' (*John* 7:30). The time for his arrest and death was not yet, and try how they might his enemies could not advance it by so much as a second. Predestination keeps perfect time. (For similar expressions to 'My hour' in John's Gospel, see also 2:4; 7:6,8; 8:20; 12:23, 27; 13:1; 16:32 and 17:1). Dr Leon Morris points out that this chain of passages in John's Gospel although unobtrusive is nevertheless convincing. John makes it clear that from the very beginning there was an appointed hour for the Saviour and before that time he could not be harmed.

Christ was well aware when his hour had not yet come. He was equally aware when it had. Thus in his great high priestly prayer he could say, 'Father, the hour has come; glorify your Son that the Son may glorify you . . .'. There is a note of finality about the perfect tense here – 'the hour has come and remains'. Yet as he prayed in the very shadow of the cross, Christ saw his death as the means to true glory, and he saw his own glory closely connected with that of his Father. Indeed they merged into one.

'So the band of soldiers . . . arrested Jesus and bound him' (*John* 18:12). In modern parlance, Christ the King was led away handcuffed. No longer had he free passage in his own world. Voluntarily he submitted to captivity – he who in all of this was to lead captivity captive! As Judas led the soldiers into the garden, the Saviour was advancing to meet him. 'Rise', he said, 'let us be going; see, my betrayer is at hand' (*Mark* 14:42). For the moment the storm had passed and Christ's whole bearing was marked by total self-possession and sublime composure. He knew what awaited him and as he went his steps were firm.

The garden was empty again, this lonely garden that time-wise is situated mid-way between Eden and a greater garden than Eden that is so beautifully described in Revelation 22, and where flows for ever 'the river of the water of life'. The struggle in Gethsemane had been fierce. Soon the struggle would be fiercer still. 'That old serpent, called the devil and Satan' had uncoiled and had bared his fangs, poised to strike again and again with all the venom of which he was capable. Trampling on serpents is a most painful experience, especially for the heel.

# 5

# THE DUMB LAMB

The high priest stood up and said, 'Have you no answer to make? What is it that these men testify against you?' But Jesus remained silent (*Matt.* 26: 62, 63).

When Christ stood before Caiaphas and the Jewish Sanhedrin, he faced the highest and most religious court in the world. Was this not an opportunity for the heavenly prophet to speak, to enter into vigorous religious discussion? Yet, to begin with, this prophet maintained a prolonged silence. Christ also stood silent before Pilate (*Matt.* 27:14) and before Herod (*Luke* 23:9). There were times when he spoke in the presence of his examiners and there were times when he held his peace. Such silence was significant and its purpose differed on each occasion. In each instance the purpose of such silence can only be determined by the context, the situation at the time.

THE ENIGMA OF CHRIST'S SILENCE

What took place in the Sanhedrin that day was more a plot than a trial. The overwhelming majority of those present had but one aim, the death of Christ. To achieve this they trampled on justice and morality. Matthew records that 'the chief priests and the whole Council were seeking false testimony against Jesus that they might put him to death' (26:59). It may well be that Joseph of Arimathea and Nicodemus were the only members of the Sanhedrin who dissented from its conduct and final verdict (*Luke* 23:50, 51, *John* 7:50–52).

It was clear from the outset that the Sanhedrin had no intention of giving the prisoner a fair trial. And so the search began for false witnesses (*Matt.* 26:59): no other kind of witness would suit their purpose! This so-called trial was a total farce. It was a travesty of justice. It represented the ultimate in hypocrisy. According to the law a person could not be condemned to death on the testimony of just one witness (*Num.* 35:30), and so these religious leaders kept scrupulously by the law! There must be more than one witness; that they should be false witnesses did not seem to trouble their conscience! William Hendriksen rightly affirms that to be tried by such men 'was in itself a deep humiliation'.

The attempt to produce witnesses proved a fiasco. There was no shortage of volunteers. Many came forward, but they failed to agree with each other and had to be dismissed. Finally two witnesses quoted the Lord's riddle about destroying the temple and raising it again within three days. But even they could not agree on the exact statement that Christ had made. One had him say, 'I am able to destroy the temple', and the other claimed that he said 'I will destroy this temple' (*Matt.* 26:61; *Mark* 14:58). So the *text* which was basic to their accusation was uncertain. That was clear for all to see. Christ could easily have confounded his accusers, for neither had quoted him correctly, and both had misunderstood his words. He did not do so, not even when the high priest sprang to his feet and demanded an answer. There certainly was considerable provocation. He would have been fully aware of prophecy being fulfilled in that meeting of the Sanhedrin. 'Give me not up to the will of my adversaries; for false witnesses have risen against me, and they breathe out violence' (*Psa.* 27:12). Such words, while expressing much of David's experience, found their ultimate fulfilment in the afflictions of great David's greater Son. Then why did the Saviour stand dumb in the presence of his accusers? Certainly it was not because he knew not what to say, or was afraid to speak.

THE REASON FOR CHRIST'S SILENCE

The charge hinged on a riddle that Christ had used when he drove out the traders and money-changers from the temple. The Jews challenged his right to do so and asked, 'What sign do you show us for doing these things?' (*John* 2:18). It was then that Christ gave them his riddle: 'Destroy this temple, and in three days I will raise it up' – a saying remembered and understood by his disciples after his resurrection. Such a teaching riddle demands an explanation. As a bare text it conveys no meaning. That is true of all riddles. However, it is of vital importance to establish the correct form of the text before a meaning can be sought. The riddle must be accurately stated. Caiaphas knew that his witnesses were not in agreement on precisely what Christ had said. The text had not been established; yet he demanded an explanation! He had abandoned the path of justice and truth. Any trumped-up charge would serve his purpose.

God does not unfold his mysteries to the wicked. The members of that Sanhedrin were not seekers after truth: they were murderers at heart. Schilder says, 'These are the birds which never pick up any seeds on the thresh- ing-floor of righteousness; they are, on the contrary, birds of prey which feed on rotten spoils.' The silent Saviour, truth incarnate, stood that day in an atmosphere heavy with intrigue, malice and corruption and that in a court of ecclesiastical dignitaries! Was this not a veritable 'syna- gogue of Satan'?

## THE SIGNIFICANCE OF CHRIST'S SILENCE

In Deuteronomy it is written, 'The secret things belong to the LORD our God, but the things that are revealed be- long to us and to our children forever . . .' (29:29). Those words were well known to the members of the Sanhedrin and the revelation concerning the Messiah contained in their Scriptures was more than adequate for their guid- ance.

Christ remained silent about the hidden things. He left his judges with the Word of God and there lay their great responsibility. They must busy themselves with the things that had been revealed. Christ will take his riddle with him to the grave. The meaning will become apparent in due course. He will not cast his pearls before swine, rather he will leave it to his judges to execute their high office before God. In this he did justice to them and at the same time condemned them.

To have explained the riddle to the Sanhedrin would not have been to the glory of God or for the good of Christ's judges. Imagine what would have happened had he said, 'Bury me and within three days I will rise again.' He would have been regarded as an ostentatious and supernatural escapologist! He would have relieved the Sanhedrin of its moral responsibility. The dawn of the New Testament Sabbath would have become the occasion for a gathering of gawping spectators hoping to see this latest wonder. What a mockery of predestination that would have been! And what a windfall for Satan! Christ the Redeemer reduced to a mere super-fakir, not lying on a bed of nails or walking on hot coals, but rising from the grave!

If Christ had explained his riddle that day, it would have been a most untimely word. That he would never do. He would not prostitute his God-given mission. All his miracles, including his resurrection, were essentially part of his kingdom and of his redeeming work. They were totally different from those related in the Apocryphal Gospels, as when it is written that the boy Jesus making clay birds with other children made his birds fly! But Christ was no magician; he had neither need nor place for stunts.

## THE MAJESTY OF CHRIST'S SILENCE

All too often Christ's silence has been given a dangerous one-sidedness, as his *passive* obedience is stressed almost, if not altogether, to the exclusion of his *active* obedience. Christ's silence was deliberate, emphatic and authoritative: it was his *deed*. The passivity of his suffering was real, but so was the activity of his obedience. Led as a lamb to the slaughter and like a sheep dumb before the shearers, he was active right up to and on the cross. He went as a king to die.

The timing, God's timing, of Christ's appearance before the Sanhedrin is noteworthy. Finlayson states that 'about the time the Paschal lambs were receiving scrutiny from the priesthood, Jesus was actually entering Jerusalem to undergo His trial, and come under the scrutiny of His earthly judges, the Lamb for our Passover'. He adds, 'And so the Levitical Priesthood sat in judgement upon the Priest of another order, the One who was Priest after the order of Melchisedec . . .'

Christ was quick to speak when his Messiahship was challenged (*Matt.* 26:64). But he never spoke in obedience to man, always in obedience to his Father and in keeping with his mission. Because of his sublime and sovereign silence, he has earned the right to speak eternally. His silence was an act of mighty obedience to his Father's will and a compliance with that wondrous mission entrusted to him in the counsels of eternity. Calvin says, 'He is now our advocate before God, always having His mouth open.' On Patmos John heard the voice of the risen Christ 'like the sound of many waters'. Hughes sees this as a reference to 'the awe-inspiring majesty of his speaking'. True; and yet his silence before the Sanhedrin was equally majestic, equally awe-inspiring. At the very heart of his redemptive work there must be seen the infinite strength of the silent Saviour. In that ecclesiastical court Satan was tempting Christ with his own riddle, twisted though it was. By a single word he might have freed himself from his enemies. But our silent Priest continued majestically to his death. O blessed silence that lay at the heart of our redemption!

The Sanhedrin finally concluded its proceedings to its own satisfaction. This holy temple, the subject of the riddle, could now be broken down, to be raised in glory. Just as the first temple was erected without sound of hammer, or any iron tool (*1 Kings* 6:7), so this temple of Christ's body will be restored in a silence that nothing can profane.

# 6

# TAKING THE OATH

And the high priest said to him, 'I adjure you by the living God, tell us if you are the Christ, the Son of God.' Jesus said to him, 'You have said so' (*Matt.* 26:63, 64).

This was the last meeting of the supreme Jewish ecclesiastical court, the Sanhedrin, warranted by God, in the sense that it could legitimately meet in his name and expect his blessing. In the counsels of heaven, once the 'curtain of the sanctuary' was 'torn in two, from top to bottom', the Sanhedrin was dismissed. In future it would be redundant. It would be left stranded in the blind alley of its wilful rejection of the truth. Historically, it was swept away with the destruction of Jerusalem in 70 AD.

This last, divinely accredited session of the Sanhedrin – a council which inherited the rich teaching and noble traditions of a great nation – met as the clock of prophecy indicated the approach of noon and the question to be decided was the question of the ages, the question put by the Saviour himself, 'Who do you say that I am?' But the Sanhedrin did not hear the ticking of that clock and had no awareness of the tension and gravity of the hour. The Christ who had refused to share the secret of his riddle with the wicked, maintaining a firm silence before

Caiaphas, when put on oath would solemnly swear that he was the Messiah, the Son of the living God.

## THE REASON FOR THIS OATH

Caiaphas was exasperated by Christ's silence. He was determined to put him to death, but his so-called witnesses had only embarrassed him. He was compelled in the end to resort to the oath, and he made use of the legal form of administering the oath that was customary in Israel. The person sworn, without repeating the form of the oath, simply answered 'Yes' or 'No'. This oath administered by the high priest was an admission that up to this moment the court had failed to concoct a charge against the Nazarene.

On one occasion the chief priests and the Pharisees met in council to consider the fact that many were believing on Jesus of Nazareth and to decide what should be done. 'If we let him go on like this, everyone will believe in him, and the Romans will come and take away both our place and our nation' (*John* 11:48). It was then that Caiaphas said, 'You know nothing at all. Nor do you understand that it is better for you that one man should die for the people, not that the whole nation should not perish.' He spoke more truly and profoundly than he realized (verses 51, 52), yet he cynically argued that it was better that one should die, however innocent, than that a whole nation should perish. His utterance was what Leon Morris terms 'a piece of cynical political realism'. How often in the affairs of nations expediency has been preferred to principle! And, alas! how often this has been the case in the courts of the church, to its incalculable loss! Not only is such expediency wrong, but also it never pays. The irony of the situation in which Caiaphas found himself was that the very thing he tried to avoid did happen! The Romans did come and did destroy both their holy place and their nation. The result of Caiaphas' counsel at that meeting of the priests and the Pharisees was the order that Jesus must be apprehended at the first opportunity. This Caiaphas now confronted Christ as his judge! Calvin well terms him 'this treacherous hypocrite'. The church historian, Dr A. M. Renwick, used to ruminate aloud in class about 'that strange creature, the wily ecclesiastic'! The godly Bishop Ryle comments that here we have 'clear proof that high ecclesiastical office exempts no man from gross errors in doctrine, and tremendous sins in practice. The Jewish priests could trace up their pedigree to Aaron, and were his lineal successors. Their office was one of peculiar sanctity, and entailed peculiar responsibilities. And yet these very men were the murderers of Christ'.

Caiaphas knew the Scriptures. He was familiar with Zechariah 6:12,13: 'Behold, the man whose name is the Branch: for he shall branch out from his place, and he shall build the temple of the LORD . . . and shall bear royal honour, and shall sit and rule on his throne.' Did Caiaphas recall those words as he looked at the prisoner? What had Jesus meant when he spoke of raising up the temple? Was it really possible that this simple Nazarene was that temple-builder, the long awaited Messiah? The true Messiah was to accomplish his work in glory. Where was the glory? How could this prisoner, abandoned by his followers and apparently helpless in the hands of his enemies, be the Messiah? To Caiaphas that was an absurdity. According to Zechariah the Messiah would unite priesthood and kingship, but every priest in Israel detested this Jesus.

Caiaphas looked at the lowly figure before him, without form or comeliness, as the world counts such, and suddenly adjured him by the name of the living God to say whether or not he was the Christ, whether or not Zechariah 6:12,13 referred to him. He demanded his credentials *on oath*. The *Westminster Confession of Faith* states, 'The name of God only is that by which men ought to swear, and therein it is to be used with all holy fear and reverence.' Considering that, as Calvin puts it, Caiaphas' mind was 'filled with malicious hatred and contempt of Christ', it is hardly an overstatement to suggest that he was guilty of taking God's Name in vain.

## THE OFFENCE OF THIS OATH

The high priest's demand added to Christ's suffering and humiliation. Those words, 'I adjure you', addressed to Christ were an insult, a subtle form of Christ-denial. The oath was only justified in exceptional cases where truth was sought, and this assembly was not seeking the truth at all! If Caiaphas had asked Christ directly if he were the Christ, he would have received a direct reply. Christ never denied his Messiahship: he often affirmed it. Demanding an oath was an affront to the integrity of his character. Tacitly Caiaphas impugned Christ's veracity. Christ knew that he was being placed on the same level as any of the sinful men around him: Speak the truth; do not perjure yourself!

Besides, Christ had a high and holy concept of the oath. It was not to be bandied about and profaned. The Jews of that time were accustomed to swearing oaths for the most trivial reasons. In home and business the most solemn oaths were used unblushingly and so the oath had lost its potency and its edge was blunted. Christ in the sermon on the mount condemned this practice. They must not swear 'by this and by that', for in each case they profaned the name of the creator. 'Let what you say be simply "Yes" or "No". . .' (*Matt.* 5:37). It is a sin to take the name of the most high God lightly. It would be a mistake, however, to conclude that Christ forbade the taking of the oath in any circumstance. The command of God is clear: 'It is the LORD your God you shall fear. Him you shall serve and by his name you shall swear' (*Deut.* 6:13). That could not be forbidden by the one who came not to 'abolish the Law or the Prophets . . . but to fulfil them', and who added, 'For truly, I say to you, until heaven and earth pass away, not an iota, not a dot, will pass from the Law until all is accomplished' (*Matt.* 5:18). The Fulfiller of the law would never have sought to annul any part of it. All God's law is inviolate.

Christ, the Truth incarnate, never spoke a word out of the context of his awareness of God. In that sense his every word was the equivalent of an oath. See, then, how grievously Caiaphas wronged and humiliated him. His demand was a denial of Christ's whole being and character. This hurt the Saviour more than all the spitting and beating that was to come. But it happened. He who was *the Truth* was put on oath to speak truly!

## THE BURDEN OF THIS OATH

Warfield reminds us that our Lord's life of humiliation 'was not His misfortune, but His achievement', and that 'He was never the victim but always the Master of circumstance'. This must be borne in mind as we reflect on the Saviour obediently taking the oath. His response was clear: 'You have said so', meaning, 'Yes indeed; I am the Christ.' It is interesting to compare Christ's response to Judas who, having heard the master speak of his betrayer, asked, 'Is it I?' Christ replied, 'You have said so' (*Matt.* 26:25). And so in Mark's account of Christ's response to Caiaphas' question, 'Are you the Christ, the Son of the Blessed?' we read, 'And Jesus said, "I am . . ."' (14:61). Caiaphas wanted a forthright 'Yes' or 'No'; he received a definite 'Yes'. The Apostle Paul, thinking of Christ's words to Pilate, spoke of his 'good' or 'beautiful' confession (*1 Tim.* 6:13). His answer to Caiaphas was worthy of the same description.

Christ was fully aware of the authority of the Sanhedrin and of his Messianic calling. He would be faithful to both. He took the oath. The burden of that oath rested equally upon Caiaphas, for those who administer the oath are also bound in the most solemn manner to behave morally. They, too, have called on God to witness their conduct and to judge them accordingly. Christ knew that his answer would lead to his death, but he made his noble confession and added, 'And you will see the Son of Man seated at the right hand of Power, and coming with the clouds of heaven'. He was echoing the words of Daniel 7:13,14, and Psalm 110:1, and applying them to himself. He saw beyond the cross and the resurrection to his glorious return as judge and he saw his enthronement at God's right hand.

In effect he was saying that when he returned the situation would be reversed. On that day his present judges would stand before his tribunal and he would be their judge! That may well have been lost on Caiaphas, but he had heard all he wanted to hear. In a mock token of dismay he rent his robe, little realizing that this was a fitting symbol of the dissolution of the typical priesthood, now that Christ the true priest had appeared!

All agreed that the prisoner was guilty of blasphemy and that he should die. They refused to acknowledge his claims. 'His own people did not receive him' (*John* 1:11). In the full light of his character, teaching and deeds, they rejected him. The cry of their hearts was, 'We do not want this man to reign over us' (*Luke* 19:14). So answers the heart of fallen man when confronted with Christ and the challenge of his cross and his crown. Never had the members of the Sanhedrin heard a proclamation so majestic as that which fell on their ears when Christ declared his Messiahship and warned of his second advent. But unbelief and prejudice blinded them to the truth.

There is no more solemn moment than when one is confronted by the Christ of God. Is he a fraud and an impostor? or is he the world's Saviour and the world's Judge?

> 'What think ye of Christ?' is the test
>  To try both your state and your scheme;
>  You cannot be right in the rest
>  Unless you think rightly of Him.

Christ's solemn oath before Caiaphas echoes throughout the centuries.

'Are you the Christ?'

'YES.'

There is the mighty rock that bears the faith of the people of God in all ages. Those who build on that foundation shall never be confounded; for the mouth of the Lord has spoken it!

# 7

# SENTENCED TO DEATH

Then the high priest tore his robes, and said, 'He has uttered blasphemy. What further  witnesses do we need? You have now heard his blasphemy. What is your judgment?' They answered, 'He deserves death' (*Matt.* 26:65, 66).

Christ's clear confession that he was the Messiah incurred the instant wrath of the Sanhedrin. The supreme ecclesiastical court of Jewry, now hurriedly convened, was suddenly swept by a storm of excitement. The confusion and uncertainty which had thus far plagued proceedings vanished, and with one voice they endorsed the indictment implicit in the high priest's words. There was no doubt in their minds as to the nature of the charge to be brought against the Nazarene.

## THE CHARGE

Blasphemy! Guilt could not be greater. The Sanhedrin could bring no charge more serious. Blasphemy was considered a graver sin than idolatry. The law was clear on the matter. 'Whoever blasphemes the name of the LORD shall surely be put to death' (*Lev.* 24:16). The blasphemer sinned most directly against God. Under Jewish law many offences were classified as blasphemy, but Christ was seen as guilty of the worst possible blasphemy when he claimed to be the Son of man and the Son of God (*Matt.* 26:64, *John* 10:36). This was not the first time that the Saviour was accused of blasphemy. He was so accused when he forgave sins (*Luke* 5:20,21) and when he affirmed that he and the Father were one (*John* 10:30,31). The Jews saw the Nazarene as an arrogant impostor, robbing God of his glory by claiming divine prerogatives (for example, forgiving sins) and even going so far as to claim equality with God. 'It is not for a good work that we are going to stone you but for blasphemy, because you, being a man, make yourself God' (*John* 10:33). Now the Sanhedrin was about to make that charge official.

Caiaphas was a polished ecclesiastic. He knew what to do and when. He knew that he was soon to preside over a meeting of the Sanhedrin in plenary session formally to confirm the verdict given. Then the court would be solemnly constituted in the name and by the authority of the God of Israel. Knowing that the prisoner was charged with an offence which deserved the holy intolerance of God, Caiaphas gave expression to his professed horror by rending his garments. As a rule the high priest was forbidden to do this (*Lev.* 10:6; 21:10), but this was no ordinary occasion. The torn clothes were meant to symbolize a broken heart, but the heart of Caiaphas was unbroken. In his heart of hearts he was glad that at last he could condemn the prisoner. He was simply acting a part. Hendriksen rightly discerns his thoughts: 'We've got him now.'

## THE EVIDENCE

Not only had Christ confessed his Messiahship, but also he had boldly declared, 'I tell you, from now on you will see the Son of Man seated at the right hand of Power and coming on the clouds of heaven' (verse 64). In other words, Christ would yet enter his glory and take his rightful place at the Father's right hand. *Here* and *now* Christ stood a bound prisoner, 'despised and rejected of men', but his eyes were on the *hereafter*. He saw beyond the cross with all its suffering and shame. The Jews, too, believed that the Messiah would be enthroned in glory, but they had come to understand this in earthly terms, and certainly did not see its fulfilment by means of suffering and death. Christ's language was unintelligible and offensive to them. They simply saw him as a self-confessed fraud and a dangerous upstart.

Is it not strange that the Jewish leaders, who were so familiar with the contents of the Old Testament Scripture, directed their criticism and derision against our Lord's prophetic and kingly roles and ignored his priestly role, a role that according to their own Scriptures was crucial in the work of the Messiah? Caiaphas overlooked this fundamental issue and, in spite of the Scriptures, gave no thought to reconciliation and satisfaction by means of suffering and death. Had he forgotten Isaiah 53? In any event he failed to see the prophecy that was being fulfilled in his presence.

If the Nazarene really were the kind of person that these religious leaders believed him to be, then their charge would have been fully justified. But was he? Was there anything in his life, teaching and ministry that did not illustrate his claims, or that conflicted in any way with righteousness and truth? Later the Apostle Peter could speak of 'Jesus of Nazareth, a man attested to you by God with mighty works and wonders and signs that God did through him in your midst, as you yourselves know . . . ' (*Acts* 2:22). These signs and works were incontrovertible. Then why should such a Person making such claims and doing such mighty works be rejected out of hand? The truth of the matter was that the Jewish leaders feared and hated this teacher who had exposed their hypocrisy, refuted their arguments and rejected their traditions. They regarded him as a threat to their authority and power. It was their intention from the outset to get rid of him by whatever means. Caiaphas' chief sin lay in his *wanting* to do what he did.

## THE SENTENCE

Death! The charade of righteous indignation was maintained, at least for a little while longer! This Nazarene must now die at the hands of pagans, for under Roman rule the Jews were not free to put a person to death. And it is important to remember that it was not just the Jews who were responsible for Christ's death. Ultimately all mankind and every person must bear full responsibility. Pilate was just as much guided by expediency as was Caiaphas. At no point did the Saviour receive justice from man. And every sinner has said in effect, 'Away with Him . . . I will not have this man to reign over me.' It was the realization of this fact that moved Horatius Bonar to write:

I see the scourges tear His back,
I see the piercing crown,
And of that crowd who smite and mock,
I feel that I am one.

'Twas I that shed the sacred blood,
I nailed Him to the tree,
I crucified the Christ of God,
I joined the mockery.

Yet not the less that blood avails,
To cleanse away my sin;
And not the less that cross prevails
To give me peace within.

The fact of universal responsibility for the rejection of Christ needs to be stressed in view of the charge repeatedly made by Jewish scholars that Christians are to blame for much of the anti-Semitism that has reared its ugly head through the centuries. There is certainly nothing in the New Testament to lend support to such an evil.

In Caiaphas' court-room the prisoner was now the object of scorn and contempt, 'a worm and no man', a blot on the very name and honour of Israel, a Philistine of the Philistines, worthy only of death. Here we touch another nerve of Christ's sufferings, his rejection by his own people. 'He came to his own, and his own people did not receive him' (*John* 1:11). He was officially disowned as a child of Abraham, he who had wept over impenitent Jerusalem. In this rejection God was rending the Saviour's heart. To be thus spurned by his own people and treated as a reprobate, was a bitter grief to bear. To be delivered to the pagans for further trial and then death added to the pain that wrenched at his heart. But the one who had come to save the world must suffer at the hands of the world.

There stands Caiaphas, his torn robe a fitting symbol of his redundancy, now that the great and everlasting high priest had come. There stands the Christ whom God introduced into the loins of Abraham and whose day Abraham by faith rejoiced to see (*John* 8:56). Now his heart is broken by a heavy grief, broken by the hand of God. 'It was the will of the LORD to crush him; he has put him to grief . . .' (*Isa.* 53:10). Before the hearts of God's elect could be broken, the Saviour's heart had to be rent with unspeakable anguish. For all who would know God's mercy in Christ the message is clear. 'Rend your hearts and not your garments' (*Joel* 2:13). 'A broken and contrite heart, O God, you will not despise' (*Psa.* 51:17).

Caiaphas has followed his declared policy – one for all. There is a strange irony here, for unwittingly the high priest was enunciating a principle that lay at the very heart of redemption. 'The Son of man came not to be served but to serve, and to give his life as a ransom for many' (*Matt.* 20:28). The Apostle Paul elaborates on this principle. 'For as by the one man's disobedience the many were made sinners, so by the one man's obedience the many will be made righteous' (*Rom.* 5:19). One for all! So another voice has spoken in Caiaphas' court. That word was spoken in the eternal counsels of the Godhead, and Christ had accepted it on behalf of those whom the Father had given to him. One for all! Did he hear that voice again as he stood condemned by the Sanhedrin?

He certainly had not forgotten it. Ultimately two voices have spoken in that courtroom, the voice of God and the voice of Satan: both said, 'One for all.' But there is fundamental disagreement between them. God speaks in terms of redemptive substitution, substitutionary atonement; Caiaphas, who is Satan's tool as much as Judas, speaks in terms of elimination. God would have his Son die for his people so that they might live; Caiaphas would have Christ die in order to be rid of him, and so he sticks by his policy that it was expedient that one man should die for the people rather than that the whole nation should perish.

Thus predestination and human responsibility meet as Christ is condemned. He was 'delivered up according to the definite plan and foreknowledge of God', yet 'crucified and killed by the hands of lawless men' (*Acts* 2:23). God's eternal purpose was realized in the death of his Son. The one for the many! So the believer can say, 'Christ embraced me with all my sin and guilt that I might embrace him in all his righteousness'. That is what Luther had in mind when he said, 'He died for me; he made his righteousness mine and made my sin his own; and if he made my sin his own, then I do not have it, and I am free.'

# 8

# THE BUTT OF MOCKERY

Then they spit in his face, and struck him. And some slapped him, saying, 'Prophesy to us, you Christ! Who is it that struck you?' (*Matt.* 26:67, 68).

The Sanhedrin adjourned from its night-time session to meet formally in the morning. It had been agreed that Christ was a blasphemer who deserved to die. To sentence someone to death is an awesome responsibility. One does not expect that judges who have passed such a sentence will almost immediately turn to revelry or frivolity. They should be burdened men. A solemn silence should pervade the courtroom. There should be a profound awareness of the majesty of the law. It is with undisguised horror that one views the monstrous spectacle in the courtyard of the high priest's palace on that momentous night. It was then that Israel's judges disgraced themselves. Scarcely had proceedings ended before their eminences threw all restraint aside and indulged in an unholy orgy of vicious abuse of the prisoner. Christ became the butt of the most diabolical mockery.

## THE CRUELTY OF THIS MOCKERY
These religious leaders, doubtless assisted by the officers and spearmen, gathered in fiendish glee around Christ

whom they saw as a worthless fraud, the object of scorn and hatred, the scum of the world. Now they would have some fun. They spat in his face, a symbol of defiance among the Jews (*Num.* 12:14, *Deut.* 25:9). They struck him repeatedly with their fists, among the Jews a token of utter contempt (*Matt.* 5:39). His face was soon bruised and swollen by the rain of heavy blows. 'His appearance was so marred, beyond human semblance, and his form beyond that of the children of mankind' (*Isa.* 52:14). Professor E. J. Young points out, 'This does not mean that he appears to be more disfigured than other men, but that his disfigurement was so great that he no longer appeared as a man.' Many who saw him were astonished (literally, 'shocked' or 'shattered'). Motyer pictures them stepping back in horror as they ask, 'Is this human?' That battered, bleeding countenance should speak mightily to all our hearts. Like all Christ's sufferings it has redemptive significance. Calvin puts it well: 'This insolence was turned by the providence of God to a very different purpose; for the face of Christ, dishonoured by spitting and blows, has restored to us that image which had been disfigured, and almost effaced, by sin.'

Suddenly the abuse took a new turn. Blindfolding the prisoner they danced around him striking him repeatedly and saying, 'Prophesy to us . . . who is it that struck you?' They knew that he had just prophesied of his future (verse 64). And so some clever wag had the bright idea of mocking the prophet from Nazareth. There he stands in nameless wretchedness as his tormentors in seeking to degrade him reveal their own degradation. Doubtless the redeemer remembered his own prophecy, 'Many bulls encompass me; strong bulls of Bashan surround me; . . . like a ravening and roaring lion' (*Psa.* 22:12, 13). Now the bulls and lions and dogs mentioned in the twenty-second Psalm close in on him, snarling and snapping in uncontrolled fury. O my soul, what a sight is this! As with tear-dimmed eyes we look on this terrible scene – do we? – we behold with wordless wonder the matchless love and infinite condescension of the one who came to seek and to save the lost.

Here, however, there is an error to avoid, the danger of seeing the loving obedience of Christ as primarily and exclusively for the sake of man, when, in fact, it was primarily out of love for God that he accepted the cross (*Heb.* 10:7). Dr Geerhardus Vos stresses that our Lord's Messiahship was 'absolutely God-centred'. 'Jesus', says Vos, 'accepted the cross out of a motive of love for God even more than, and before, He accepted it because of His love for man.' And again Vos says, 'In dying, as in all else He did, He hallowed God's name.' This is a truth too often overlooked, and it in no way detracts from the wonder that Christ loves each one of his people with all of his love.

As that suffering, humiliated figure stood there, his tormentors despised him in their hearts. They thought that he was utterly helpless in their hands. How wrong they were! Christ was never in retreat, never merely passive. At this moment he was actively and voluntarily exposing himself to the fury of his enemies. Now came the fulfilment of those prophetic words, 'I gave my back to those who strike, and my cheeks to those who pull out the beard; I hid not my face from disgrace and spitting' (*Isa.* 50:6). This was costly obedience on the Saviour's part as he deliberately gave his back to those who struck him, enduring patiently and meekly this gratuitous torture. E. J. Young says, 'There is majesty in the description, as though the servant were in full control of the situation. He sets himself forth as one who acts.'

Just as Caiaphas spoke more profoundly than he realized when he said that it was better that one should die than that they all should perish, so Christ's tormentors must have struck a chord in the Saviour's mind as they chanted, 'Who is it that struck you?' Many hands were raised against him, both human and demonic, but Christ knew that there was one hand above all others that smote him. And as he bore our sins that hand did not spare him. 'It was the will of the LORD to bruise him; he has put him to grief . . .' (*Isa.* 53:10).

## THE SIGNIFICANCE OF THIS MOCKERY

Christ in his passion was mocked on several occasions and each time the mockery occupied a unique place in his experience. First he was mocked by Israel, next he was mocked by the pagan world, then by a descendant of Edom, a false brother, and finally by all these together. He was mocked by the Sanhedrin, by Pilate's soldiers, by Herod and then by them all as they stood before the cross. So the mockery in the presence of the Sanhedrin had its own special features. Its focal point was Christ's prophetic role, an office now openly derided. Little did his enemies realize that every detail of his suffering was a fulfilment of prophecy, even the crowing of a rooster! As Schilder remarks, 'It had to crow because God wrenched the creature's beak wide open . . .'. Even as the members of the Sanhedrin mocked the Messiah, he stood at the very summit of the mountain of prophecy. The prophetic altitude of this mountain will only be matched on the day of judgement.

In the midst of this gruesome abuse our Lord stood unflinchingly, leaving himself at the mercy of his enemies, he who by a word could have destroyed them. But he maintained the omnipotence of his silence. 'When he was reviled, he did not revile in return; when he suffered, he did not threaten; but continued entrusting himself to him who judges justly' (*1 Pet.* 2:23). Says that fine 17th-century expositor, Alexander Nisbet, 'While Christ our Lord was suffering in our room He did with much confidence and willingness deliver Himself to the will of His righteous Father to endure the utmost that was due to sinners, according to his undertaking in the covenant of redemption.' Consider the magnitude of the task in hand that required so terrible a cost. In his bearing in the midst of vile abuse, the Saviour left us an example that we should follow his steps. We cannot be faithful to Christ in this world and avoid reproach and contempt, and in this our bearing should correspond in some measure to that of the master when he was so defamed. It is well to remember the words of Samuel Rutherford, 'The worst things of Christ, His reproaches, His cross, are better than Egypt's treasures.'

## THE SOURCE OF THIS MOCKERY

Sometimes mockery is justified. Elijah mocked the prophets of Baal, exposing the impotence of their god, even as the Psalmist mocked the idols with mouths that could not speak, eyes that could not see, and ears that could not hear (*Psa.* 115). The cartoonist mocks what he sees as foolish government policy or public behaviour and in doing so renders a useful service to society. Mockery *per se* is not wrong. Even God mocks (*Psa.* 2:4). But unrestrained mockery that is unrelated to God's holy law becomes undiluted brutality. It is wholly destructive, particularly of the mocker himself. Such mockery is a form of defiance and behind this defiance of the Christ one senses the presence of the demonic.

All hostility to Christ and his people is stimulated by the powers of darkness. The Apostle Paul was acutely aware of those vicious demonic forces of which the persecuting State was but the instrument. The struggle was not with flesh and blood, but with 'the authorities . . . the cosmic powers . . . the spiritual forces of evil' (*Eph.* 6:12). Therefore believers needed to be clad in 'the armour of God'. The battle was with the forces of Satan, and it was those same forces that launched this cruel assault against the Son of God in the high priest's courtyard, and the sufferer knew full well who it was that assailed him.

Throughout his earthly life Christ never suffered for himself, and for a sinless being to move in the sin-laden atmosphere of this fallen world meant intense suffering. The Christian winces when he hears the name of his beloved Saviour used in profane jest, yet in many ways all Christians fail to be as sensitive to the presence of evil as they should be. But the sinless one was totally sensitive to the presence of evil. We must not, therefore, limit his redemptive sufferings to the last few days of his life before the crucifixion and to his actual agony on the cross. William Symington rightly affirms, 'In every case He suffered for us, never for Himself'; and he adds, 'Not one throb of pain did He feel, not one pang of sorrow did He experience, not one sigh of anguish did He heave, not one tear of grief did He shed for Himself. If not one of His sufferings was personal, it follows that they were all substitutionary . . .'. During the whole period of his [earthly] life the Saviour 'was a-slaying'.

How terrible was that mockery of Christ by the Sanhedrin! How godless! Had Christ not been thrust outside the sphere of law, such contempt and unbridled abuse would have been impossible. If his judges had been sincere in their assessment of the prisoner, and in the verdict they reached, and if they had feared God, they would have delivered the accused to Satan that he might learn not to blaspheme (*1 Tim.* 1:20). That would have been a *lawful* and a *loving* act, but the Sanhedrin had no regard for either justice or love. Lawlessness and hatred are boon companions. And so the Saviour was treated as an arch-liar, a worm to be trampled under foot, someone to be put for ever without the domain of law. For the one who had God's law in his heart and who delighted to do God's will, to be thus ejected from the sphere of justice meant intense suffering of spirit, for him an agony that far surpassed the pain inflicted by physical abuse. And so those

# 9

# THE CROWN OF THORNS

Then came Jesus forth, wearing the crown of thorns
(*John* 19:5, KJV).

The Sanhedrin having sat informally at night and declared Christ guilty of blasphemy and deserving of death, met formally in the early hours of the following morning to pronounce the sentence of death and then hurried the prisoner to Pilate the Roman governor who alone could confirm the sentence and order its execution.

Although in some respects Pilate was more honourable than Caiaphas, in that he clearly recognized and acknowledged the innocence of Christ, nevertheless he was weak and vacillating as the Jewish leaders clamoured for Christ's death. When Pilate tried to release Christ, the Jewish leaders cried out, 'If you release this man you are not Caesar's friend'. He was trapped by his own past, his bad administration. 'Shall I crucify your King?' he asked, and they replied, 'We have no king but Caesar.' Pilate was cornered. He knew that they could appeal to Caesar and then there would be an investigation of his administration. He recognized the veiled threat their words conveyed and he bowed to their demands. 'So he delivered him over to them to be crucified' (*John* 19:12, 15, 16).

Like Caiaphas, Pilate had put expediency before principle and again the irony of the situation becomes apparent, for the very outcome he tried to avoid did take place; a complaint was lodged against him; it is reported that he was deposed and banished and finally committed suicide. However we view his sin, it is not as great as that of the chief priests who had the Scriptures and the evidence of Christ's light and teaching and yet hated him without a cause.

Behind the scenes the soldiers have had their fun with the prisoner. Having heard that he claimed to be a king, they dressed him in a purple robe, possibly a soldier's red cloak, made a crown of thorns and put it on his head, placing a reed in his hand for a sceptre. This parody continued as they bowed in mock obeisance saying, 'Hail, King of the Jews!', smiting him and spitting on him and striking him repeatedly on the head with the stiff reed that served as sceptre (*Matt.* 27:28–30). Godet is probably right when he sees this mockery addressed more to the Jewish nation, despised by the Romans, than to Christ personally. But that did not detract from the suffering and abuse resulting from this rough horse-play. The rendering of John 19:5 in the King James Version points to that dramatic moment when Christ was brought forth for all to see: '*Then* came Jesus forth, wearing the crown of thorns.' That sad spectacle left its mark for ever on John's mind.

## THE SHAME OF THIS CROWN

There he stood, his face bruised, swollen and bleeding, and that thorny crown upon his head. He was so alone, 'friendless, forsaken, betrayed by all'. That crown symbolized what sinful man thinks of Christ. He was not to be taken seriously. He was only fit for a stage-play! They made him a carnival king and placed on him the stamp of derision. With this mock robe, reed sceptre and crown of thorns, he was made to look like a theatrical figure. Luther says that Christ was 'numbered with the transgressors, crucified as a rebel, killed by His own people in supreme disgrace, and as the most abandoned of men'. Ah yes! 'supreme disgrace', the shameful crown of thorns woven by the hands of men and placed on the Saviour's brow – *man's estimate of Christ!*

Christians may well be troubled and moved by this sight. Not so the crowd outside Pilate's palace. As Pilate pointed to that battered, bleeding figure saying, 'Behold the man!' he hoped for some pity, some compassion, but he hoped in vain. That sight only served to heighten their lust for blood. Had he not suffered enough? Did this not satisfy them? Could this pathetic figure really be a threat to them? But all that smote Pilate's ears was the steady chanting of 'Crucify, Crucify' (there is no 'him' in the original) – a veritable crescendo of angry voices. What cries greeted the Saviour in those few eventful days! Hosanna! Hosanna! . . . Crucify! Crucify! They could not bear the light of the world; they felt more at ease in the darkness of deception and hypocrisy. As Krummacher says, they could not endure 'the broad daylight of unvarnished truth'. The Holy One of Israel exposed them, unmasked them, condemned them and they turned against him with vicious hatred and a consuming desire to destroy him. They would give no glory to this Jesus, no honour, nothing but shame and contempt. The crown of thorns pleased them well. That is the response of the heart of fallen man to the Lord's Christ. Nothing has changed. 'The rulers take counsel together, against the LORD and against his anointed, saying, "Let us burst their bonds apart and cast their cords from us"' (*Psa.* 2:2,3).

## THE SIGNIFICANCE OF THIS CROWN

There is its significance for *a lost world*. Christ came to be the Saviour of the world and that meant enduring the cross with all its shame and suffering. That crown of thorns was placed there by God as well as by man. The cross was God's cross as well as man's.

If we are to receive the crown of life, Christ must receive the crown of thorns. He cannot be our Saviour any other way. That is what Krummacher means when he comments that in the crown of his deity alone, Christ could only say to a dying thief, 'Be thou accursed'; but in the crown of thorns he can say, 'This day shalt thou be with me in Paradise.' In the crown of his deity alone, he can only say to a Magdalene or a publican, 'Depart from me'; but in the crown of thorns he can say, 'Go in peace, your sins are forgiven you.' It is in his diadem of thorns that he stoops low in humiliation and shame and sorrow to seek and to save sinners. It is only by the sharp thorn of his suffering that the poisonous thorn of our sin is drawn. In other words, apart from the cross God cannot forgive sin.

There is also the significance of the crown of thorns for *the church*, for God's redeemed people. It reminds us

that Christ is a king and that he *is* victorious even when
he seems defeated. However abased Christ may appear to
men he is still a king. He accomplishes a regal task at Calvary and gains for us a royal pardon. He ascends a throne
as he goes to be crucified, a throne of grace. In this apparent weakness he is the mighty conqueror of Satan and sin
and death, the overcomer of this world. The cross appears
as foolishness to the world, but to God's redeemed people
that cross is victory, salvation, the power of God.

## THE WONDER OF THIS CROWN

Matthew Henry speaks of 'the invincible patience' of our
Saviour. Certainly behind that crown of thorns worn for
us we see invincible patience and invincible love – a love
that we can never understand, but which, by God's grace,
we may experience. Only unspeakable love, unquench-
able love, divine love could wear *that* crown of thorns;
and that is the wonder of it. Some lines by Christina
Rossetti are apposite.

> I bore with thee long weary days and nights,
> Through many pangs of heart, through many tears,
> I bore with thee, thy hardness, coldness, slights,
> For three-and-thirty years.

> I bore thee on My shoulders and rejoiced.
> Men only marked upon My shoulders borne
> The branding cross; and shouted hungry-voiced,
> Or wagged their heads in scorn.

> A thief upon My right hand and My left;
> Six hours alone, athirst, in misery:
> At length in death one smote My heart and cleft
> A hiding-place for thee.

Pilate's *Ecce Homo*, 'Behold the man!', still rings in our ears. And in faith we do behold him. Then he was presented as a ludicrous figure, a caricature of royalty. Only the eye of faith can see the wonder of God's grace in such circumstances. Dr James Stalker writes, 'How little Pilate understood his own words! That "Ecce Homo" of his sounds over the world and draws the eyes of all generations to that marred visage. And lo, as we look, the shame is gone; it is lifted off Him and fallen on Pilate himself, on the soldiery, the priests, and the mob. His out-flashing glory has scorched away every speck of disgrace, and tipped the crown of thorns with a hundred points of flaming brightness.' The brow that once wore the cruel crown of thorns is now adorned with the diadem of the universe, for all authority in heaven and on earth has been given to Christ. 'We see Jesus . . . crowned' (*Heb.* 2:9). 'Behold, the Lamb of God, who takes away the sin of the world!' (*John* 1:29).

# 10

# OUTSIDE THE GATES

So they took Jesus, and he went out, bearing his own cross, to the place called the place of a skull, which in Aramaic is called Golgotha (*John* 19:17).

*V*ia dolorosa! Those Latin words describe the horror of that dreadful walk that the Saviour took as he staggered beneath his cross to the place where he was to die. He had been surrounded by a web of intrigue, falsehood and injustice, and that where truth was supposed to be enthroned and justice honoured! Yet not only did he submit to the injustice of his accusers, but also he submitted to the justice of God which he had come to satisfy. They stood in balance and tension, the injustice of man and the justice of God. From the human side there was nothing but injustice, yet in a manner beyond our understanding God's judgment was executed by means of the evil deeds of men (*Acts* 2:23).

CHRIST THE OUTLAW

From the time of his arrest Christ was denied justice. His judges virtually placed him beyond the pale of law and treated him accordingly. That was so with Herod, the

Sanhedrin and Pilate. Between them he was little more than a pawn to be pushed back and forth to suit their own ends. Condemnation in the different courts was not based on evidence; indeed it defied evidence. Pilate confessed, 'I did not find this man guilty of any of your charges against him. Neither did Herod . . . Look, nothing deserving death has been done by him . . .' (*Luke* 23:14,15). Yet, at the end of the day, a cowardly governor released Barabbas, guilty of insurrection and murder, and yielded to the demand of Christ's accusers! Christ was 'delivered over to their will' (*Luke* 23:25).

So much for justice! From the outset Christ was in no man's land, and no man's land was any man's land in that anyone could treat the prisoner as he pleased. There was no legal protection. Justice stood afar off. Truth was fallen in the street. Equity could not enter. In reality Christ was placed beyond law. Christ the outlaw!

In a just society everyone lives in the context of law and has a right to the law's protection. Condemnation must be in the context of law; but Christ was condemned outside the sphere of law when justice was openly discarded. Cain was given a sign to protect him from lawlessness. His place within the province of law was guaranteed. That privilege was denied Christ. He, the Just One, knew the pain of being denied every shred of justice.

## CHRIST THE ACCURSED

Christ felt both the hurt of man's injustice and the weight of God's justice as he went forth to bear the full curse of sin and so to be accursed of God. He was to die on a cross and 'cursed is every one that hangeth on a tree' (*Gal.* 3:13, KJV). Paul quotes from Deuteronomy 21:22, 23. The law required that the body of an executed criminal should hang on a post, but should not be left there overnight. 'A hanged man', it declared, 'is accursed of God.' To be thus hanged on a tree was considered the greatest possible disgrace and the most shameful end for any man, being publicly proclaimed to be under God's curse. Matthew Henry comments, 'Those that see him thus hang between heaven and earth will conclude him abandoned of both and unworthy of either.' The Christ who redeemed his people from the curse of the law was himself made a curse for them, and hanging on a tree proclaimed that awful fact, for in ancient Israel those punished in the manner described in Deuteronomy 21 were not accursed because they were hanged on a tree, but conversely they were hanged on a tree because they were accursed.

In the light of Galatians 3:13, the ancient law prescribing the hanging of the executed on a tree is seen as a symbol and type of Christ's curse-bearing at Calvary, as in similar manner the brazen serpent on the pole foreshadowed the cross. Calvin says, 'It was not unknown to God what death his own Son would die, when he pronounced the law, "He that is hanged is accursed of God".' It is interesting to note the use of the term 'tree' in the book of Acts (5:30; 10:39; 13:29). The word in the original means wood and Peter uses it on two occasions. It is most likely that he had Deuteronomy 21:23 in mind and his Jewish hearers would immediately appreciate the force of his words. Peter was making the point that the

Lord Jesus Christ had borne our curse; he was not dodging the 'scandal' of the cross, on the contrary, twice he reminded his hearers that Christ was 'hanged on a tree'.

The Apostle Paul is relentless in his application of this prophetic passage in Deuteronomy 21. Christ, he says, became 'a curse for us', even as elsewhere he says that Christ was 'made . . . to be sin for us'. He bore our sin and its consequences, even the curse of a holy God. He was treated as if he were a sinner. God's curse is intrinsically holy. It is his condemnation of sin and the sinner. It is his mighty *action* against sin and it is instant in its effect. Christ *as sin-bearer* was inevitably accursed of God. Just as blessing reaches its fullness in heaven, so the curse reaches its fullness in hell, and Christ experienced the curse in its fullness.

By God and man alike, but for different reasons, Christ was driven outside the gates, the scapegoat laden with sins. Part of the ritual of the Day of Atonement necessitated 'a sin offering' for which two male goats were used. One goat was slain, the other sent into the wilderness after the high priest had laid his hands on its head confessing as he did so the sins of the people. 'The goat shall bear all their iniquities on itself to a remote area . . .' (*Lev.* 16:22). That goat was presented there as a symbolical substitute in a ceremony of absolution. Symbolically the now-atoned-for sins were laid on him to be removed for ever out of sight. Those two goats were essential to the symbolism of that *one sin offering* (verse 5). One goat exhibited the *means*, the other the *effect* of the atonement. So Christ in his own Person and work actually offered himself as a sacrifice for the sins of his people, sins that the Father had laid on him, thereby removing them for ever out of sight (see *Isa.* 38:17, *Jer.* 31:34; *Mic.* 7:19), but the cost was incalculable, the burden crushing and the curse as bitter as hell.

## CHRIST THE SURETY

A surety, in personal terms, is one who becomes bound for another. It was as Surety for his people that Christ went to the place of the curse as one condemned. It was as Surety that he went to pay their debt in full. It was thus that he bore the chastisement that made them whole. For Christ the pains of hell which others experience *after* death must be endured *before* death, not in the next world, but in this. So man's injustice, which defied all human logic, was in keeping with God's logic, and man's crooked dealings became the vehicle of divine justice, paradoxical as it is to human reason. It was, therefore, as Surety that Christ was 'made a curse', was 'made sin' and consequently driven outside the gates, those gates through which he had passed so recently on the foal of an ass with loud hosannas ringing in his ears! Now he was sent to the place of the unclean. Jerusalem's refuse dump, itself a lurid symbol of hell, was also outside the gates. Josiah appointed the vale of Hinnom, once a centre of gross idolatry, as a rubbish dump, a place where offal was burnt and where the fires never went out (2 *Kings* 23:10). Gehinnom, or Gehenna, is translated 'hell' in the Bible and Christ frequently used the name in that sense, referring to hell (Gehenna) as a place 'where their worm does not die, and the fire is not quenched' (*Mark* 9:48, see also *Isa.* 66:24). Whatever was unclean was taken outside the holy city. The carcases of animals offered as sacrifices on the Day of Atonement were to be burned *outside the camp* (*Lev.* 16:27). Citing this, the writer to the Hebrews continues, 'So Jesus also suffered outside the gate in order to sanctify the people through his own blood. Therefore let us go to him outside the camp, and bear the reproach for him' (*Heb.* 13:12, 13).

## CHRIST THE OUTCAST

To say that Christ suffered outside the camp in order to sanctify the people through his own blood was a stunning statement for Jewish readers. It was shocking to be told that Christ made his great sacrifice on what they considered unholy ground, outside the camp. In ancient Israel when a man left the camp he needed ceremonial cleansing before he could return (*Lev.* 16:26). How, then, could Christ sanctify his people on unsanctified and profane ground? The holy city, however, had been defiled at the time of Christ's trial, defiled as never before. In Moses' day, when Israel had incurred God's wrath by using the golden calf in worship, a 'tent of meeting' was erected some distance from the camp. We read in Exodus 33:7, 'Everyone who sought the LORD would go out to the tent of meeting, which was *outside the camp*.' What had happened? Israel had defiled the holy ground *within* the camp, so that those who sought the Lord must go outside the camp. Sin had rendered the camp unholy, so the situation was reversed: *inside* the camp was unholy, but God's presence in the temporary sanctuary *outside* the camp made that place holy. It was sacred because of God's presence.

What happened at Jerusalem in our Lord's day was an exact parallel of the situation confronting Moses. By the iniquity of Christ's trial and the ill-treatment meted out to him, the holy city had been grossly defiled. Now the old values were reversed. What had been sacred was now unhallowed and what had been unhallowed was now hallowed. The presence of the Saviour consecrated what had been profane. It was fitting and right that he should offer himself a sacrifice for our sins outside the gates. Now, there is no further need for 'holy places' for the worship of God, nor in God's sight can there be such.

Little did those who led the Saviour outside the city walls to Golgotha realize the significance of their action. To them the prisoner must be ejected from their midst. Outside the gates! Christ the untouchable!

He must not remain in what they considered the domain of holiness. This blasphemer, this impostor must be cast out. Nothing so unclean must be allowed to defile Jerusalem's holy ground. That is how they saw it; that is how they *wanted* to see it. Their rejection of Christ was total. Christ, however, had to die at Jerusalem, the city of the Word. No other city would have done. It was the only place in the economy of redemption where the lamb of God could die outside the gates as one accursed of God. As the priests hustled Christ outside the gates, they ministered, in spite of themselves, to the preparation of the one and final sacrifice for sin. Jerusalem was the only place: the Passover was the only time. 'For Christ, our Passsover lamb, has been sacrificed. Therefore let us keep the Festival . . .' (*1 Cor.* 5:7,8, NIV). 'What remains now', says Calvin, 'is that we eat, not once a year, but continually.'

Outside the gates! An outcast in God's universe! No resting place, no sanctuary! But not for long. Soon the gates of heaven will swing wide for the warrior Christ.

> Lift up your heads, O gates!
> And be lifted up, O ancient doors,
> that the King of glory may come in.
>
> *Psalm 24:7*

# SATAN'S CUP REFUSED

And they offered him wine mixed with myrrh; but he did not take it (*Mark* 15.23).

Everything in Christ's earthly life was significant. Whether eating or drinking, he did all to the glory of God. In the fullest sense his food was to do the will of his Father. The cup that the Father gave him, he would drink. The cup of demons he would refuse. That was his law in life and in death.

## THE UNMIXED CUP

The cup that the Father placed in the Son's hands was brimful of wrath and judgement. Its every drop brought torment. Yet *this cup* he would drink to the glory of God! This cup he would drink in honour of God's holiness and righteousness. This cup of death he would drink in order that not one of his people might ever taste a single drop of it. 'Shall I not drink the cup that the Father has given me?' (*John* 18:11). Yes, indeed! He would drink it to its dregs. He would drain that cup. Not one drop would be left. When he asked his disciples, 'Are you able to drink the cup that I drink?' (*Mark* 10:38), he was indicating an action already begun. Dr W. L. Lane suggests that the use of the present tense would support the translation, 'Can you drink the cup that I am in the process of drinking?'

Not only would the Saviour drink the cup of divine wrath, with its steadily increasing bitterness, but also, in terms of his suffering, he would drink no other cup, nor would he accept any admixture. He would drink the cup that the Father had given him *unmixed*. Not a solitary drop of any other potion must blend with that prepared by the Father. That cup must be kept pure. He must drink it as it was poured out by God. Only thus could he drink it to the glory of God and only thus could he drink it savingly for his people. God's cup of wrath is essentially unmixed, that is *undiluted* (*Rev.* 14:10). Dilute that cup with a single extraneous drop and it is no longer the cup of God's wrath. For that matter, add one foreign ingredient to the cup of God's mercy and it ceases to be such. God's wrath and God's mercy alike are unmixed.

## THE DRUGGED CUP

It was customary, by way of preparation for crucifixion, to offer the condemned a sedative drink. Mark says that Christ was offered 'wine mixed with myrrh' (15:23). Matthew speaks of 'wine . . . mixed with gall' (27:34). The word translated 'gall', like 'marah' in the Old Testament, can be used broadly of something which is bitter. Thus in the Septuagint (the Greek translation of the Old Testament) the word for gall is used in the same sense, and in Deuteronomy 32:32, KJV, we read, 'Their grapes are grapes of gall, their clusters are bitter.'

This narcotic drink was offered for the purpose of deadening the pain. Matthew in his account was probably thinking of Psalm 69:21a, 'They put gall in my food . . .' (NIV). Dr J. A. Alexander remarks that 'the passion of our Lord was providentially so ordered as to furnish a remarkable coincidence with this verse'. It must not be forgotten that, in the final analysis, it is Christ who speaks prophetically in this great passion Psalm.

The soporific mixture offered to the Saviour was immediately refused. As soon as he tasted it he realized what it was (*Matt.* 27:34). A drink to quench his thirst would have been welcome, and he did accept such a drink (verse 48). That sour wine he accepted, but the drugged drink he instantly refused. To the very last he must have full possession of his senses. As A. H. Strong observes, his cry of dereliction on the cross 'was not an ejaculation of thoughtless or delirious suffering'. Nothing must be allowed to insulate his spirit from the reality of the situation. Spurgeon remarks, 'He solemnly determined that to offer a sufficient atoning sacrifice He must go the whole way, from the highest to the lowest, from the throne of highest glory to the cross of deepest woe.' He must suffer to the utmost. He must feel the full 'sting' of his death. No anaesthetic was permissible. In Mark's account of this incident the Greek text would suggest that they persisted in offering this drink to Christ and consequently he repeatedly refused it.

THE SATANIC CUP

The apparently innocent cup offered to Christ had a sinister origin. Even as he tasted the sedative he recognized the hand of the tempter. Mocked, scourged, worn out as he staggered to Golgotha beneath the burning sun, he craved a cool draught to quench his raging thirst. The tempter said, 'Drink! This will cool your tongue.' Satan knew that the one about to be crucified was the Messiah. He did not understand, however, the mystery of his Person, the union, without fusion, of the divine and the human: only God himself understands that mystery. Nor did Satan appreciate the fact that a divine Person cannot sin. Christ saw the situation in a flash. He refused Satan's cup. He was about to descend into even greater depths of suffering as he experienced the unmitigated wrath of a holy God against sin and as he grappled with the legions of darkness that were hurled against him. In that hell not so much as a drop of water may cool his tongue, nor relieve in the smallest degree his agony.

What if Christ had accepted that cup (and that is to imagine the impossible)? Then, with a befuddled brain, he could not have prayed for the soldiers who were waiting to nail him to the cross. Then those seven great sayings on the cross would never have been uttered. Then his obedience would at last have been broken and all would have been lost. How much was at stake as they pushed the rim of that cup towards the Saviour's lips! Everything! All of the divine decree, all of prophecy, all of redemption was at stake as that appealing cup was offered to the suffering one again and again.

Adam had *disobeyed* knowingly, with all his senses clear. The 'last Adam' must obey willingly and with a clear mind. No wonder Schilder says that 'the refusal of the cup of myrrh is just as important as the shedding of Jesus' blood'. The Christ of God could not and did not waver. He knew that he must endure the cross. The world, as Schilder points out, had 'a sword in one hand and a soothing cup in the other', but God held 'a sword in one hand and a sword in the other'.

The great High Priest, offering the once-for-all sacrifice for sin, must know what he does, must in no way be insensible or inattentive. In this crucial encounter with Satan the Saviour must not be doped, nor must he allow the emphasis to shift from the realm of the spirit to that of the body. The body must subserve the spirit, not *vice versa*. Viewed from every conceivable angle, this was Satan's cup. His fingermarks were all over it. The fetid stench of his breath still clung to it. Christ pushed it away. He spurned it with all his being. He drank only from the Father's cup and now he hands to each one of the redeemed that precious cup that overflows with the sweet wine of his love, the cup of salvation.

THE FUTURE CUP

There was another cup which our Lord declined, the fourth cup at the Passover when he instituted the holy supper. The four cups were understood in terms of the four-fold promise of Exodus 6:6, 7: 'I will bring you out . . . I will deliver you from slavery to them . . . I will redeem you . . . I will take you to be my people, and I will be your God.' That fourth cup which the Saviour declined was the cup of consummation and fulfilment. He therefore said, 'I tell you I will not drink again of this fruit of the vine until that day when I drink it new with you in my Father's kingdom' (*Matt.* 26:29). The expression *'that day'* points us to the age to come when that which is now incomplete will be 'new', that is, fulfilled. The term *'new'* in the New Testament so often has the meaning of consummation.

Christ did not drink from that sacramental cup or eat of that sacramental bread, but he clearly saw their redemptive significance. Herman Ridderbos sees the relationship between the Supper and eating and drinking with Christ in glory as 'not merely that between symbol and reality, but that between commencement and fulfilment'. We need to recapture the awareness of this when we come to the Lord's table. Again it becomes plain that Christ never doubted the outcome of his passion as he looked on that red wine, symbolic of a violent death. He knew that he would drink from the cup of complete fulfilment with his redeemed in the kingdom of God and at 'the marriage supper of the Lamb'. No other cup must come between his present cup of suffering and that blessed cup that awaited him and his own.

As we take the sacramental cup in our hands, may we be profoundly conscious that this is a foretaste of that heavenly banquet. Our thoughts might well be of the cup Christ drank, the cup he refused, and the cup from which he will drink with us in glory.

# 12

# THE KING AMONG BANDITS

And when they came to the place that is called The Skull, there they crucified him, and the criminals, one on his right and one on his left (*Luke* 23:33).

There is a stark contrast between Christ's coming into the world in the presence of the Magi, God-fearing shepherds and a few devout worshippers in the temple, and his death in the company of bandits. It must be remembered, however, that he died as he had lived, in the midst of sinners. 'His position symbolically set forth the significance of His death', as Leon Morris aptly says. Christ willingly submitted to the most cruel and degrading form of punishment known to man, described by Josephus as 'the most wretched of all ways of dying'. How marvellous was this mighty submission of the Lord!

> Twelve legions girded with angelic sword
> Were at his beck, the scorned and buffeted:
> He healed another's scratch; his own side bled,
> Side, feet, and hands, with cruel piercings gored.
> Oh wonderful the wonders left undone!
> And scarce less wonderful than those he wrought;
> Oh self-restraint, passing all human thought,
> To have all power, and be as having none;

> Oh self-denying love, which felt alone
> For needs of others, never for its own.

Thus Archbishop R. C. Trench reflects on one aspect of Christ's obedience.

At times one may wonder at the almost matter-of-fact way in which the evangelists describe the crucifixion of the Saviour. They do not dwell, as many have done since, on the horrors of this form of death; the emphasis is not on the physical aspect of Christ's sufferings. Great as the physical agony of Christ undoubtedly was, it is unlikely that on the cross he suffered more in this sense than did those crucified with him. His physical agony was as nothing in comparison to his spiritual suffering. That is why the Gospels direct our attention to what the Lord endured as our sin-bearer.

## THE MOCKERY OF PILATE

It was common practice to display a placard listing the crimes of a person condemned to crucifixion. Pilate had this 'title' placed over Christ's head, 'Jesus of Nazareth, the King of the Jews.' By this he was deliberately taunting the Jews. He was not concerned to revile the crucified One, whom he knew to be innocent, but rather to insult the Jews. His placard repeated his earlier words, 'Shall I crucify your King?' and the Jews were cut to the quick by his calculated insult. Pilate had poured all the disdain and sarcasm of which he was capable into that inscription. He was saying in effect, 'Look, you Jews, here is your king!' What a king! this battered, bleeding, crucified figure! Pilate was relishing this mockery, for the Jews had exasperated him that day and his revenge was sweet, in spite of the stirrings of his enfeebled conscience. But then, taking the line of least resistance makes rivers and men crooked! It is not difficult to imagine Pilate's sardonic smile and heartless laugh as he read his inscription: *Jesus the Nazarene, the King of the Jews!* INRI: *Jesus Nazarenus Rex Judaeorum).*

Pilate was mocking the Jews to his heart's content as he crucified the Nazarene among the lowest criminals, with this title above his cross. The man who asked bitterly, 'What is truth?', cared nothing for ethical integrity as he deliberately placed Christ on a par with malefactors. The Saviour would have been keenly aware of what Pilate was about and although he had suffered unspeakable abuse at the hands of his own people, he would inwardly weep for them, even as he had wept over Jerusalem. Pilate's bitter taunt gave him no satisfaction; indeed his whole being must have opposed it, for God had a great future for Abraham's seed. Pilate might sneer at the Jews, but not Christ. 'Has God rejected his people? By no means! . . . God has not rejected his people whom he foreknew' (*Rom.* 11:1, 2). The Jews would be indignant at Pilate's taunt, but the Saviour, understanding its intent, felt its sting even more.

## THE COMPANIONS OF CHRIST

The all important thing at Calvary was not the action of Pilate, but that of God. Everything here, as elsewhere, was firmly grounded in predestination. Christ's companions in death and his place in their midst resulted from

God's ordering of events. Christ knew that. As his cross was jolted into place between the malefactors, he knew that this was exactly where he was meant to be. A short time previously he had said to his disciples, 'For I tell you that this Scripture must be fulfilled in me. "And he was numbered with the transgressors." For what is written about me has its fulfillment' (*Luke* 22:37). So on his cross Christ knew that the word through Isaiah had come to pass: 'He was numbered with the transgressors.' It was not the first time that he had been so reckoned, and that by his own insistence, when he was baptized in the Jordan. Then, as now, he was fully and freely identified with sinners, for such he came to save.

In no way did the Lord resent being placed among such men at Calvary. The quotation from Isaiah 53:12 may literally be translated, 'He . . . let himself be numbered with the transgressors'. He was totally content with his position; he would not have had it otherwise. He knew that his place among these bandits was willed by his Father and his Father's will was his will. These criminals, placed there by God, were appropriate company at this time for his Son.

Here, too, is the mystery of divine sovereignty and human responsibility (*Acts* 2:23), those parallel lines that to our finite minds never meet. Those who try to make them meet succeed only in distorting both. It is possible, but by no means certain, that in heaven the parallel lines in question will be seen from a different perspective. In this life they must not be tampered with. They are both true and that is enough. Let the people of God praise him that his Son was so placed at Calvary. Let it be maintained that Christ died not just as the representative of his people, but *in their stead,* dying their death that they might live. In a word, he died as their Substitute.

## THE ELECTION OF GRACE

Golgotha was not far from Zion, the symbol of communion, and Gehenna, the symbol of perdition! At Golgotha one was taken and the other left. Pilate's levelling process had no validity in the sight of God. Pilate might despise Israel and seek to cast her off, but God has not and will not cast off his people. As in the time of Elijah, 'There is a remnant according to the election of grace' (*Rom.* 11:5, KJV), and that gracious election was evident at Calvary where one criminal experienced that circumcision of heart that characterizes the true seed of Abraham (*Rom.* 2:28,29) - *one* that no one might despair, and *only one* that no one might presume! Thus, on his cross, the Saviour called a guest to the wedding feast. Finlayson puts it movingly: 'He has a right to take a guest home with Him without asking leave of any. He had the key to the Father's door in His pierced hand. He could open and no man shut. He could shut and no man open, and the guest He took home with Him to His Father's table that day was the first trophy of Calvary after the sacrifice had been finished.' Reflecting on those in the vicinity of the cross, Finlayson adds, 'I would rather be in the shoes of Barabbas. Barabbas had a wonderful angle on the cross; he could point to the middle cross and say, "There would I have been, if He had not been put in my place".'

Predestination and election! They are clearly in evidence here. God's judgments are unfathomable and his ways untraceable (*Isa.* 55:8,9). Many baulk at this. They make themselves the measure of what God should be and do – God made in man's image! Let them listen to the voice of God. 'Who are you, O man, to answer back to God?' (*Rom.* 9.20). 'Even so, Father; for so it seemed good in thy sight' (*Luke* 10:21, KJV). John Murray comments that 'when dealing with the determinate will of God, we have an ultimate on which we may not interrogate him nor speak back when he has uttered his verdict. Who are we to dispute his government?'

Numbered with the transgressors! *There* is comfort and hope for the greatest sinner who repents. Let God's people bow humbly before the cross and marvel at the fact that any should find mercy. Let each one say, '*Why me?*' Is there any reason apart from the grace of God?

> Home of our hearts, lest we forget
> What our redemption meant for Thee,
> Let our most reverent thought be set
> Upon Thy Calvary.

Not the proud and arrogant thought, but, as Amy Carmichael puts it, 'most reverent thought' befits the sinner before the cross. As we stand in thought before that cross our emotions are mixed. How dreadful and yet how wondrous is this place! John Bunyan expresses our feelings well.

> Thus far did I come laden with my sin;
>  Nor could aught ease the grief that I was in
> Till I came hither: What a place is this!

Must here be the beginning of my bliss?
Must here the burden fall from off my back?
Must here the strings that bound it to me crack?
Blest Cross! blest Sepulchre! blest rather be
The Man that there was put to shame for me.

'Jesus of Nazareth, King of the Jews.' Pilate, like Balaam of old, prophesied in spite of himself. Involuntarily and unwittingly he witnessed to the truth. What he wrote, God had written first. As the jeering crowds read that placard they began to chant, 'If he be the King of Israel, let him now come down from the cross, and we will believe him' (*Matt.* 27:42, KJV). The Royal Conqueror, however, went on to victory. In apparent weakness and defeat, he reigned from his cross. He is the King of Israel, not just of the Jews, but of all who believe in him, the true Israel of God (*Gal.* 3:29; 6:16). Let the redeemed of the Lord say, 'Thou art the Son of God; thou art the King of Israel', and let those letters stand for ever: *INRI.*

## 13

# OUTER DARKNESS

Now from the sixth hour there was darkness over all the
land until the ninth hour (*Matt.* 27:45).

Christ on his cross was still the butt of ridicule. The
chief priests with the scribes and elders led the
rabble in this mockery. Boldly they taunted him. 'He
saved others; he cannot save himself. He is the King of
Israel; let him come down now from the cross, and we
will believe in him.' Then, suddenly, it grew dark! The
silence was eerie; just the occasional splatter of blood on
the stones, or the crunch of a soldier's step. The terrible
picture of suffering and humiliation faded from view.
And what a scene that was!

> I asked the heavens, — 'What foe to God hath done
> This unexampled deed?' — The heavens exclaim,
> ''Twas man; and we in horror snatched the sun
> From such a spectacle of guilt and shame.'

True: but that is not the whole story.

## THE SINGULARITY OF THIS DARKNESS

At high noon, when the sun was at its zenith, Christ
and those who stayed to mock found themselves in thick

darkness that was to last for three hours. A hand from on high had veiled the sun. Cowed but not convinced, the scoffers grew silent and slunk away. As Calvin says, they were 'bewitched by the enchantments of Satan'.

At Bethlehem, when the Saviour was born, the night was changed to day as the glory of the Lord shone around the shepherds. On Golgotha the day gave way to night as Christ sank deeper and deeper into the abyss of damnation. At Bethlehem there were countless angels praising God; on Golgotha legions of darkness filled the impenetrable gloom, hoping that darkness would finally triumph over light.

Golgotha was so different from the mount of transfiguration where the Lord conversed with Moses, representing the law, and Elijah, representing the prophets (*Mark* 9:2–4). There, for a brief moment, the glory of deity broke through the veil of flesh, a fleeting glimpse of the radiant splendour of Christ when he comes at the end of this age 'in the glory of his Father with the holy angels' (*Mark* 8:38).

Between the shining forth of glory at the transfiguration and the glory of the second coming, however, lies the heavy darkness of Golgotha.

At the creation, God, at an early stage, introduced light. Yet now he leaves his Son suspended in darkness at midday. Why must the light of the world be placed in darkness? Why is there this startling contrast between Bethlehem and Golgotha, between the transfiguration and Golgotha, between the dawn of creation and that of the new creation?

## THE SIGNIFICANCE OF THIS DARKNESS

Not only did this darkness at noonday hide the awful spectacle of the Sufferer from the contemptuous gaze of the scoffers, silencing their ribaldry, but also it mercifully concealed Christ when he experienced his darkest moment on the cross. No human eye must see him then. *This darkness coincided with Christ's descent into hell.* Now he felt the unmitigated wrath of a holy God against sin. That darkness was a symbol of God's wrath. Hendriksen says that God's wrath was 'burning itself out in the heart of Jesus', adding, 'Hell came to Calvary that day, and the Saviour descended into it and bore its horrors in our stead.' This was the Passover season. Just before the first Passover a plague of darkness betokened the curse of God upon his enemies (*Exod.* 10:21–23). The darkness that enveloped the Saviour at Calvary was clearly a visible expression of the inner darkness that wrung that dread cry of dereliction from his lips: 'My God, my God, why have you forsaken me?' (*Matt.* 27:46). To be forsaken by God is hell.

This was the moment when the prophecy of Daniel 9:26 was fulfilled: 'An anointed one shall be cut off, and shall have nothing' (see also *Isa.* 53:8). E. J. Young sees the expression 'shall have nothing' (literally 'and there is not to him') as 'a very forceful way of setting forth His utter rejection, both by God and man . . . In that hour of blackness He had nothing, nothing but the guilt of sin of all those for whom He died. Utterly forsaken, He was cut off'. Frans Bakker has this in mind when he thinks of Christ on the cross, poor and naked as the day he was born, while the soldiers gambled for his clothing. 'Not only did He lose all His gifts; He also lost the Giver. But He didn't cry about His condition, only that God had forsaken Him. Christ cried to God, but for Him there was no mercy; He had to bear the curse; He had no rights.' This is the stunning truth, yet, paradoxically, in the very moment that he lost all, he won all. As the Apostle Paul considered Christ's death on the cross, the thought suddenly struck him, 'He did it because he loved me' – another stunning truth.

*This darkness was equally symbolical of Christ's struggle with the powers of darkness.* After all, this was their hour (*Luke* 22:53) when they were free to do their worst. The ecclesiastics who indulged in jeers and cruel jests were only the tools of those sinister forces of darkness. The blotting out of the sun should have made those earthly dignitaries stop and think. When God plunged Egypt into darkness, Goshen had light. Now men groped to find their way in Jerusalem! Where was their Goshen now? Those men, however, missed the message of the darkness. They did not repent. In that darkness, not merely the physical darkness, but rather that 'outer darkness', Christ battled with Satan and his legions and triumphed gloriously. C. H. Spurgeon says, 'The present battle in which you and I take our little share is as nothing compared with that wherein all the powers of darkness in their dense battalions hurled themselves against the almighty Son of God. He bore their onset, endured the tremendous shock of their assault, and in the end, with shout of victory, He led captivity captive.'

*The darkness at Calvary is also a reminder of creation's 'sympathy' with its Lord.* It was fitting that the sun should be darkened when the Creator went to the cross, there to suffer in his human nature. Creation, in every atom and cell, is totally dependent on Christ for its existence. 'He is before all things, and in him all things hold together' (*Col.* 1:17). He is the Sustainer as well as the Creator of the universe. Scripture stresses the sympathy that exists between Christ and the world of nature, and the bond that there is between creation and man himself. Thus creation is represented as in birth pangs, waiting for its deliverance 'from the bondage of corruption into the glorious liberty (or, liberty of the glory) of the children of God' (*Rom.* 8:21–22, KJV). Just as creation was radically affected by man's sin, so it will share in the glory to be bestowed upon the children of God. There will be cosmic regeneration (*Eph.* 1:10, *Col.* 1:20). 'It was inevitable', says J. N. Geldenhuys, 'that the world of nature, the creation of God through the Son (*John* 1:3), should on that day be radically affected.' Darkness! Earthquake! Rent rocks! Small wonder, then, that the Psalms associate the joy of creation with the coming of Christ at the last day (for example, *Psa.* 96:11–13).

*Darkness also symbolizes mystery.* There is much mystery at Calvary. A great deal has been revealed: substitution, conflict with the evil one, reconciliation and more – God's holiness, justice and love. But how much of any of these can the human mind grasp? Is not Calvary a place veiled in darkness, even as God himself dwells in thick darkness (*1 Kings* 8:12, *Psa.* 18:11), a place so holy and so awful that the wisest thing to do is to remove one's shoes and bow in penitent, grateful silence?

## THE PORTENT OF THIS DARKNESS

This darkness, charged as it was with divine judgment, signalled the final judgment. And again darkness is used as a symbol of God's wrath. The Apostle Peter, quoting from the prophet Joel, declared, 'The sun shall be turned to darkness and the moon to blood, before the day of the Lord comes, the great and magnificent day' (*Acts* 2:20; see *Isa.* 13:10; 50:3, *Joel* 2:30, 31, *Amos* 8:9). Barely two months previously the people of Jerusalem had seen the sun turned into darkness, and, as F. F. Bruce points out, 'The paschal moon may well have appeared blood-red in the sky in consequence of that preternatural gloom.' These signs were tokens of the day of judgment, and so the prophecy of Joel forms the background to the description of the day of wrath in Revelation 6:12, 'And the sun became black as sackcloth, the full moon became like blood . . .'. There we see the doom of the godless as this day of grace comes to an end, and all is for ever dark.

Did the light begin to return when Christ uttered his awful cry of God-forsakenness? Certainly it was then that they could see to dip a sponge in vinegar and give it to him to drink (*Matt.* 27:48). Then was fulfilled the Lord's own prophecy, 'For my thirst they gave me sour wine to drink' (*Psa.* 69:21) — a cheap, sour wine to quench his burning thirst. That darkness had held eternity in every minute that passed. It has been urged that because Christ's sufferings were temporal and not eternal they could not be an equivalent for the eternal punishment of the lost. It is further asked how the death of one man could possibly be a satisfaction for the sins of an incalculable multitude. Such objections do not sufficiently take into account the fact that while Christ suffered in his human nature, he was a divine Person. Because of the infinite dignity of the One who suffered, there was infinite value attached to his work.

If the darkness through which the Saviour passed was so dreadful, how great must be the darkness of the sin he bore. This, says Calvin, should 'excite in us deeper horror at our sins'. Those who live and die in unforgiven sin, live and die in darkness. There is no light for anyone except in Christ. Earthly wisdom is darkness in the sight of God. Christ exclaimed, 'If then the light in you is darkness, how great is the darkness!' (*Matt.* 6:23). Calvin comments, 'Christ has good grounds for declaring that thick and appalling darkness must of necessity reign in the life of men, when they choose to be blind.' It is Christ who by his cross turns man's night into day. Spurgeon says, 'The cross is the lighthouse which guides poor weather-beaten humanity into the harbour of peace.'

When the Covenanter, John Welsh, was imprisoned in a dungeon in Blackness, on the Firth of Forth, he received a letter from Lady Melville, of Culross, addressed to him and his fellow-captives, bidding them to be thankful that they were only 'in the darkness of Blackness, and not in the blackness of darkness'. Christ spoke solemnly of 'outer darkness', associating it with unspeakable anguish (*Matt.* 8:12; 22:13; 25:30). To redeem his people

# EPILOGUE

As in thought and experience we stand before the cross, we tremble as we consider the wrath of God which flames forth against his Son. We tremble, too, when we think of the sin which incurred such fearful judgement – *our sin*. Here the awakened soul can only cry out, 'God be merciful to me *the* sinner.' That is all we dare ask for. Here and nowhere else abundant mercy is found. Christina Rossetti had it right –

> None other Lamb, none other Name,
> None other Hope in heaven or earth or sea,
> None other Hiding-place from guilt and shame,
> None besideThee.

The proud, self-sufficient, modern humanist despises the whole idea of forgiveness. Like the blustering W. E. Henley, he sees himself as master of his fate and captain of his soul. 'Forgiveness', said George Bernard Shaw, 'is a beggar's refuge. We must pay our debts.' About the time of Luther's death, a piece of paper was found in his pocket on which he had written in Latin and German, '*Hoc est verum. Wir sind alle Bettler.*' ('This is true. We are all beggars.') There is the contrast between the stony heart of unbelief and the heart of flesh that weeps for sin and looks in faith to the crucified and risen Saviour for mercy.

The forgiven, restored sinner willingly takes up his cross and follows the Lord Jesus Christ. That cross is whatever the Christian suffers for the sake of Christ and his truth. In bearing that cross there is peace and blessedness as the Christian experiences the fellowship of Christ's sufferings. Not that we can share in the redemptive suffering of Christ, but rather that we seek by God's grace to deny self, accept the anguish of the struggle against sin and bear meekly the scorn of a world that rejects Christ. 'There are some', said Samuel Rutherford, 'who would have Christ cheap. They would have Him without the cross. But the price will not come down.'

The hand that reaches out for salvation must be empty. Everything of self must be disowned. We are debtors to mercy alone. We are all beggars.

# Dear Ijeawele

A Feminist Manifesto
in Fifteen Suggestions

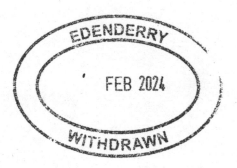

Also by Chimamanda Ngozi Adichie

# Dear Ijeawele

## A Feminist Manifesto
## in Fifteen Suggestions

Chimamanda Ngozi Adichie

4th ESTATE • London

4th Estate
An imprint of HarperCollins*Publishers*
1 London Bridge Street
London SE1 9GF
www.4thEstate.co.uk

First published in Great Britain in 2017 by 4th Estate
This 4th Estate paperback edition published 2018
First published in the United States in 2017 by Alfred A. Knopf,
a division of Penguin Random House LLC

This is a slightly expanded version of a letter written by
the author as a Facebook post on 12 October 2016

4

Printed and bound in Great Britain by
CPI Group (UK) Ltd, Croydon

**MIX**
Paper from
responsible sources
FSC
www.fsc.org
**FSC** C007454

This book is produced from independently certified FSC paper
to ensure responsible forest management

For more information visit: www.harpercollins.co.uk/green

*For Uju Egonu.*
*And for my baby sis, Ogechukwu Ikemelu.*
*With so much love.*

# Dear Ijeawele

A Feminist Manifesto
in Fifteen Suggestions

# Introduction

When a couple of years ago a friend of mine from childhood, who'd grown into a brilliant, strong, kind woman, asked me to tell her how to raise her baby girl a feminist, my first thought was that I did not know.

It felt like too huge a task.

But I had spoken publicly about feminism and perhaps that made her feel I was an expert on the subject. I had over the years also helped care for many babies of loved ones; I had worked as a babysitter and helped raise my nephews and nieces. I had done a lot of watching and listening, and I had done even more thinking.

In response to my friend's request, I decided to write her a letter, which I hoped would be honest and practical, while also serving as a map of sorts for my own feminist thinking. This book is a version of that letter, with some details changed.

Now that I, too, am the mother of a delightful baby girl, I realize how easy it is to dispense advice about raising a child when you are not facing the enormously complex reality of it yourself.

Still, I think it is morally urgent to have honest conversations about raising children differently, about trying to create a fairer world for women and men.

My friend sent me a reply saying she would 'try' to follow my suggestions.

And in rereading these as a mother, I too am determined to try.

# Dear Ijeawele,

What joy. And what lovely names: Chizalum Adaora. She is so beautiful. Only a week old and she already looks curious about the world. What a magnificent thing you have done, bringing a human being into the world. 'Congratulations' feels too slight.

Your note made me cry. You know how I get foolishly emotional sometimes. Please know that I take your charge – how to raise her feminist – very seriously. And I understand what you mean by not always knowing what the feminist response to situations should be. For me, feminism is always contextual. I don't have a set-in-stone rule; the closest I have to a formula are my two 'Feminist Tools' and I want to share them with you as a starting point.

The first is your premise, the solid unbending belief that you start off with. What is your premise? Your feminist premise should be: I matter. I matter equally. Not 'if only'. Not 'as long as'. I matter equally. Full stop.

The second tool is a question: can you reverse X and get the same results?

For example: many people believe that a woman's feminist response to a husband's infidelity should be to leave. But I think staying can also be a feminist choice, depending on the context. If Chudi sleeps with another woman and you forgive him, would the same be true if you slept with another man? If the answer is yes, then your choosing to forgive him can be a feminist choice because it is not shaped by a gender inequality. Sadly, the reality in most marriages is that the answer to that question would often be no, and the reason would be gender-based – that absurd idea of 'men will be men', which means having a much lower standard for men.

I have some suggestions for how to raise Chizalum. But remember that you might do all the things I suggest, and she will still turn out to be different from what you hoped, because sometimes life just does its thing. What matters is that you try. And always trust your instincts above all else, because you will be guided by your love for your child.

Here are my suggestions:

## First Suggestion

Be a full person. Motherhood is a glorious gift, but do not define yourself solely by motherhood. Be a full person. Your child will benefit from that. The pioneering American journalist Marlene Sanders, who was the first woman to report from Vietnam during the war (and who was the mother of a son), once gave this piece of advice to a younger journalist: 'Never apologize for working. You love what you do, and loving what you do is a great gift to give your child.'

I find this to be so wise and moving. You don't even have to love your job; you can merely love what your job does for you – the confidence and self-fulfilment that come with doing and earning.

It doesn't surprise me that your sister-in-law says you should be a 'traditional' mother and stay home, that Chudi can afford not to have a double-income family.

People will selectively use 'tradition' to justify anything. Tell her that a double-income family is actually the true Igbo tradition because not only did mothers farm and trade before British colonialism, trading was exclusively done by women in some parts of Igboland. She would know this if reading books were not such an alien enterprise to her. OK, that snark was to cheer you up. I know you are annoyed – and you should be – but it is really best to ignore her. Everybody will have an opinion about what you should do, but what matters is what you want for yourself, and not what others want you to want. Please reject the idea that motherhood and work are mutually exclusive.

Our mothers worked full-time while we were growing up, and we turned out well – at least you did; the jury is still out on me.

In these coming weeks of early motherhood, be kind to yourself. Ask for help. Expect to be helped. There is no such thing as a Superwoman. Parenting is about practice – and love. (I do wish, though, that 'parent' had not been turned into a verb, which I think is the root of the global middle-class phenomenon of 'parenting' as one endless, anxious journey of guilt.)

Give yourself room to fail. A new mother does not necessarily know how to calm a crying baby. Don't assume that you should know everything. Read books, look things up on the Internet, ask older parents, or just use trial and error. But above all, let your focus be on remaining a full person. Take time for yourself. Nurture your own needs.

Please do not think of it as 'doing it all'. Our culture celebrates the idea of women who are able to 'do it all' but does not question the premise of that praise. I have no interest in the debate about women 'doing it all' because it is a debate that assumes that care-giving and domestic work are singularly female domains, an idea that I strongly reject. Domestic work and care-giving should be gender-neutral, and we should be asking not whether a woman can 'do it all' but how best to support parents in their dual duties at work and at home.


## Second Suggestion

Do it together. Remember in primary school we learned that a verb was a 'doing' word? Well, a father is as much a verb as a mother. Chudi should do everything that biology allows – which is everything but breastfeeding. Sometimes mothers, so conditioned to be all and do all, are complicit in diminishing the role of fathers. You might think that Chudi will not bathe her exactly as you'd like, that he might not wipe her bum as perfectly as you do. But so what? What is the worst that can happen? She won't die at the hands of her father. Seriously. He loves her. It's good for her to be cared for by her father. So look away, arrest your perfectionism, still your socially conditioned sense of duty. Share child care equally. 'Equally' of course depends on you both, and you will have to work it out, paying equal attention to each person's needs. It does not have to mean a literal fifty-fifty or a day-by-day score-keeping but you'll know when the child-care work is equally shared. You'll know by your lack of resentment. Because when there is true equality, resentment does not exist.

And please reject the language of help. Chudi is not 'helping' you by caring for his child. He is doing what he should. When we say fathers are 'helping', we are suggesting that child care is a mother's territory, into which fathers valiantly venture. It is not. Can you imagine how many more people today would be happier, more stable, better contributors to the world, if only their fathers had been actively present in their childhood? And never say that Chudi is 'babysitting' – people who babysit are people for whom the baby is not a primary responsibility.

Chudi does not deserve any special gratitude or praise, nor do you – you both made the choice to bring a child into the world, and the responsibility for that child belongs equally to you both. It would be different if you were a single mother, whether by circumstance or choice, because 'doing it together' would then not be an option. But you should not be a 'single mother' unless you are truly a single mother.

My friend Nwabu once told me that because his wife left when his kids were young, he became 'Mr Mum', by which he meant that he did the daily care-giving. But he was not being a 'Mr Mum'; he was simply being a dad.

## Third Suggestion

Teach her that the idea of 'gender roles' is absolute nonsense. Do not ever tell her that she should or should not do something because she is a girl.

'Because you are a girl' is never a reason for anything. Ever.

I remember being told as a child to 'bend down properly while sweeping, like a girl'. Which meant that sweeping was about being female. I wish I had been told simply, 'bend down and sweep properly because you'll clean the floor better'. And I wish my brothers had been told the same thing.

There have been recent Nigerian social media debates about women and cooking, about how wives have to cook for husbands. It is funny, in the way that sad things are funny, that we are still talking about cooking as some kind of marriageability test for women.

The knowledge of cooking does not come pre-installed in a vagina. Cooking is learned. Cooking – domestic work in general – is a life skill that both men and women should ideally have. It is also a skill that can elude both men and women.

We also need to question the idea of marriage as a prize to women, because that is the basis of these absurd debates. If we stop conditioning women to see marriage as a prize, then we would have fewer debates about a wife needing to cook in order to earn that prize.

It is interesting to me how early the world starts to invent gender roles. Yesterday I went to a children's shop to buy Chizalum an outfit. In the girls' section were pale creations in washed-out shades of pink. I disliked them. The boys' section had outfits in vibrant shades of blue. Because I thought blue would be adorable against her brown skin – and photograph better – I bought one. At the checkout counter, the cashier said mine was the perfect present for the new boy. I said it was for a baby girl. She looked horrified. 'Blue for a girl?'

I cannot help but wonder about the clever marketing person who invented this pink-blue binary. There was also a 'gender-neutral' section, with its array of bloodless greys. 'Gender-neutral' is silly because it is premised on the idea of male being blue and female being pink and 'gender-neutral' being its own category. Why not just have baby clothes organized by age and displayed in all colours? The bodies of male and female infants are similar, after all.

I looked at the toy section, which was also arranged by gender. Toys for boys are mostly active, and involve some sort of doing – trains, cars – and toys for girls are mostly passive and are overwhelmingly dolls. I was struck by this. I had not quite realized how early society starts to invent ideas of what a boy should be and what a girl should be.

I wished the toys had been arranged by type, rather than by gender.

Did I ever tell you about going to a US mall with a seven-year-old Nigerian girl and her mother? She saw a toy helicopter, one of those things that fly by wireless remote control, and she was fascinated and asked for one. 'No,' her mother said. 'You have your dolls.' And she responded, 'Mummy, is it only dolls I will play with?'

I have never forgotten that. Her mother meant well, obviously. She was well versed in the ideas of gender roles – that girls play with dolls and boys with helicopters. I wonder now, wistfully, if the little girl would have turned out to be a revolutionary engineer, had she been given a chance to explore that helicopter.

If we don't place the straitjacket of gender roles on young children, we give them space to reach their full potential. Please see Chizalum as an individual. Not as a girl who

18

should be a certain way. See her weaknesses and her strengths in an individual way. Do not measure her on a scale of what a girl should be. Measure her on a scale of being the best version of herself.

A young Nigerian woman once told me that she had for years behaved 'like a boy' – she liked football and was bored by dresses – until her mother forced her to stop her 'boyish' interests. Now she is grateful to her mother for helping her start behaving like a girl. The story made me sad. I wondered what parts of herself she had needed to silence and stifle, and I wondered about what her spirit had lost, because what she called 'behaving like a boy' was simply behaving like herself.

Another acquaintance, an American living in the Pacific Northwest, once told me that when she took her one-year-old son to a baby playgroup, where babies had been brought by their mothers, she noticed that the mothers of baby girls were very restraining, constantly telling the girls 'don't touch' or 'stop and be nice', and she noticed that the baby boys were encouraged to explore more and were not restrained as much and were almost never told to 'be nice'. Her theory was that parents unconsciously start very early to teach girls how to be, that baby girls are given less room and more rules and baby boys more room and fewer rules.

Gender roles are so deeply conditioned in us that we will often follow them even when they chafe against our true desires, our needs, our happiness. They are very difficult to unlearn, and so it is important to try to make sure that Chizalum rejects them from the beginning. Instead of letting her internalize the idea of gender roles, teach her self-reliance. Tell her that it is important to be able to do for herself and fend for herself. Teach her to try to fix physical things when they break. We are quick to assume girls can't do many things. Let her try. She might not fully succeed, but let her try. Buy her toys like blocks and trains – and dolls, too, if you want to.

# Fourth Suggestion

Beware the danger of what I call Feminism Lite. It is the idea of conditional female equality. Please reject this entirely. It is a hollow, appeasing and bankrupt idea. Being a feminist is like being pregnant. You either are or you are not. You either believe in the full equality of men and women or you do not.

Feminism Lite uses analogies like 'he is the head and you are the neck'. Or 'he is driving but you are in the front seat'. More troubling is the idea, in Feminism Lite, that men are naturally superior but should be expected to 'treat women well'. No. No. No. There must be more than male benevolence as the basis for a woman's well-being.

Feminism Lite uses the language of 'allowing'. Theresa May is the British prime minister and here is how a progressive British newspaper described her husband: 'Philip May is known in politics as a man who has taken a back seat and allowed his wife, Theresa, to shine.'

*Allowed.*

Now let us reverse it. Theresa May has allowed her husband to shine. Does it make sense? If Philip May were prime minister, perhaps we might hear that his wife had 'supported' him from the background, or that she was 'behind' him, or that she'd 'stood by his side', but we would never hear that she had 'allowed' him to shine.

*Allow* is a troubling word. *Allow* is about power. You will often hear members of the Nigerian chapter of the Society of Feminism Lite say, 'Leave the woman alone to do what she wants as long as her husband allows.'

A husband is not a headmaster. A wife is not a schoolgirl. Permission and being allowed, when used one-sidedly – and they are nearly only used that way – should never be the language of an equal marriage.

Another egregious example of Feminism Lite: men who say 'Of course a wife does not

22

always have to do the domestic work, I did domestic work when my wife travelled.'

Do you remember how we laughed and laughed at an atrociously written piece about me some years ago? The writer had accused me of being 'angry', as though 'being angry' were something to be ashamed of. Of course I am angry. I am angry about racism. I am angry about sexism. But I recently came to the realization that I am angrier about sexism than I am about racism.

Because in my anger about sexism, I often feel lonely. Because I love, and live among, many people who easily acknowledge race injustice but not gender injustice.

I cannot tell you how often people I care about – men and women – have expected me to make a case for sexism, to 'prove' it, as it were, while never having the same expectation for racism. (Obviously, in the wider world, too many people are still expected to 'prove' racism, but not in my close circle.) I cannot tell you how often people I care about have dismissed or diminished sexist situations.

Like our friend Ikenga, always quick to deny that anything is caused by misogyny, never interested in listening or engaging, always eager to explain how it is in fact women who are privileged. He once said, 'Even though the general idea is that my father is in charge at our home, it's my mother who is really in charge behind the scenes.' He thought he was refuting sexism, but he was making my case. Why 'behind the scenes'? If a woman has power then why do we need to disguise that she has power?

But here is a sad truth: our world is full of men and women who do not like powerful women. We have been so conditioned to think of power as male that a powerful woman is an aberration. And so she is policed. We ask of powerful women – is she humble? Does she smile? Is she grateful enough? Does she have a domestic side? Questions we do not ask of powerful men, which shows that our discom-

24

fort is not with power itself, but with women. We judge powerful women more harshly than we judge powerful men. And Feminism Lite enables this.

## Fifth Suggestion

Teach Chizalum to read. Teach her to love books. The best way is by casual example. If she sees you reading, she will understand that reading is valuable. If she were not to go to school, and merely just read books, she would arguably become more knowledgeable than a conventionally educated child. Books will help her understand and question the world, help her express herself, and help her in whatever she wants to become – a chef, a scientist, a singer, all benefit from the skills that reading brings. I do not mean school books. I mean books that have nothing to do with school, autobiographies and novels and histories. If all else fails, pay her to read. Reward her. I know this remarkable Nigerian woman, Angela, a single mother who was raising her child in the United States; her child did not take to reading so she decided to pay her five cents per page. An expensive endeavour, she later joked, but a worthy investment.

## Sixth Suggestion

Teach her to question language. Language is the repository of our prejudices, our beliefs, our assumptions. But to teach her that, you will have to question your own language. A friend of mine says she will never call her daughter 'princess'. People mean well when they say this, but 'princess' is loaded with assumptions, of a girl's delicacy, of the prince who will come to save her, etc. This friend prefers 'angel' and 'star'.

So decide for yourself the things you will not say to your child. Because what you say to your child matters. It teaches her what she should value. You know that Igbo joke, used to tease girls who are being childish – 'What are you doing? Don't you know you are old enough to find a husband?' I used to say that often. But now I choose not to. I say, 'You are old enough to find a job.' Because I do not believe that marriage is something we should teach young girls to aspire to.

Try not to use words like 'misogyny' and 'patriarchy' too often with Chizalum. We feminists can sometimes be too jargony, and jargon can sometimes feel too abstract. Don't just label something misogynistic; tell her why it is, and tell her what would make it not be.

Teach her that if you criticize X in women but do not criticize X in men, then you do not have a problem with X, you have a problem with women. For X please insert words like anger, ambition, loudness, stubbornness, coldness, ruthlessness.

Teach her to ask questions like: what are the things that women cannot do because they are women? Do these things have cultural prestige? If so, why are only men allowed to do the things that have cultural prestige?

It is helpful, I think, to use everyday examples.

Remember that television commercial we watched in Lagos, where a man cooks and his wife claps for him? True progress is when she doesn't clap for him but just reacts to the food itself – she can either praise the food or not praise the food, just as he can praise hers or not praise hers, but what is sexist is that she is praising the fact that he has undertaken the act of cooking, praise that implies that cooking is an inherently female act.

Remember the mechanic in Lagos who was described as a 'lady mechanic' in a newspaper profile? Teach Chizalum that the woman is a mechanic, not a 'lady mechanic'.

Point out to her how wrong it is that a man who hits your car in Lagos traffic gets out and tells you to go and bring your husband because he 'can't deal with a woman'.

Instead of merely telling her, show her with examples that misogyny can be overt and misogyny can be subtle and that both are abhorrent.

Teach her to question men who can have empathy for women only if they see them as relational rather than as individual equal humans. Men who, when discussing rape, will always say something like 'if it were my daughter or wife or sister'. Yet such men do not need to imagine a male victim of crime as a brother or son in order to feel empathy. Teach her, too, to question the idea of women as a special species. I once heard an American politician, in his bid to show his support for women, speak of how women should be 'revered' and 'championed' – a sentiment that is all too common.

Tell Chizalum that women actually don't need to be championed and revered; they just need to be treated as equal human beings. There is a patronizing undertone to the idea of women needing to be 'championed and revered' because they are women. It makes me think of chivalry, and the premise of chivalry is female weakness.

## Seventh Suggestion

Never speak of marriage as an achievement. Find ways to make clear to her that marriage is not an achievement, nor is it what she should aspire to. A marriage can be happy or unhappy, but it is not an achievement.

We condition girls to aspire to marriage and we do not condition boys to aspire to marriage, and so there is already a terrible imbalance at the start. The girls will grow up to be women preoccupied with marriage. The boys will grow up to be men who are not preoccupied with marriage. The women marry those men. The relationship is automatically uneven because the institution matters more to one than the other. Is it any wonder that, in so many marriages, women sacrifice more, at a loss to themselves, because they have to constantly maintain an uneven exchange? One consequence of this imbalance is the very shabby and very familiar phenomenon of two women publicly fighting over a man, while the man remains silent.

When Hillary Clinton was running for president of the United States, the first descriptor on her Twitter account was 'Wife'. The first descriptor on the Twitter account of Bill Clinton, her husband, is 'Founder', not 'Husband'. (Because of this, I have an unreasonable affection for the very few men who use 'husband' as their first descriptor.) In a strange way, it doesn't feel unusual that she would define herself as a wife like this, while he doesn't define himself as a husband. It feels normal, because it is so common; our world still largely values a woman's marital and maternal roles more than anything else.

After she married Bill Clinton in 1975, Hillary Clinton kept her name, Hillary

Rodham. Eventually she began to add his name, Clinton, to hers and then after a while she dropped Rodham because of political pressure – because her husband would lose voters who were offended that his wife had kept her name.

Reading of this made me think not only of how American voters apparently place retrograde marital expectations on women, but also of my own experience with my name.

You remember how a journalist unilaterally decided to give me a new name – Mrs Husband's Surname – on learning that I was married, and how I asked him to stop because that was not my name. I will never forget the smouldering hostility from some Nigerian women in response to this. It is interesting that there was more hostility, in general, from women (than from men), many of whom insisted on calling me what was not my name, as though to silence my voice.

I wondered about that, and thought that perhaps for many of them, my choice represented a challenge to their idea of what is the norm.

Even some friends made statements like: 'You are successful and so it is OK to keep your name.' Which made me wonder: why does a woman have to be successful at work in order to justify keeping her name?

The truth is that I have not kept my name because I am successful. Had I not had the good fortune to be published and widely read, I would still have kept my name. I have kept my name because it is my name. I have kept my name because I like my name.

There are people who say, 'Well, your name is also about patriarchy because it is your father's name.' Indeed. But the point is simply this: whether it came from my father or from the moon, it is the name that I have had since I was born, the name with which I travelled my life's milestones, the name I have answered to since that first day I went to kindergarten in Nsukka on a hazy morning and my teacher said, 'Answer "present" if you hear your name. Number one: Adichie!'

More important, every woman should have the choice of keeping her name – but the reality is that there is an overwhelming societal pressure to conform. There are obviously women who want to take their husband's name, but there are women who do not want to conform yet for whom the required energy – mental, emotional, even physical – is just too much. How many men do you think would be willing to change their name on getting married?

'Mrs' is a title I dislike because Nigerian society gives it too much value. I have observed too many cases of men and women who proudly speak of the title of Mrs as though those who are not Mrs have somehow failed at something. Mrs can be a choice, but to infuse it with as much value as our culture does is disturbing. The value we give to Mrs means that marriage changes the social status of a woman but not that of a man. (Is that perhaps why many women complain of married men still 'acting' as though they were single? Perhaps if our society asked married men to change their names and take on a new title, different from Mr, their behaviour might change as well? Ha!) But more seriously, if you, a twenty-eight-year-old master's degree holder, go overnight from Ijeawele Eze to Mrs Ijeawele Udegbunam, surely it requires not just the mental energy of changing passports and licences but also a psychic change, a new 'becoming'? This new 'becoming' would not matter so much if men, too, had to undergo it.

I prefer Ms because it is similar to Mr. A man is Mr whether married or not, a woman is Ms whether married or not. So please teach Chizalum that in a truly just society, women should not be expected to make marriage-based changes that men are not expected to make. Here's a nifty solution: each couple that marries should take on an entirely new surname, chosen however they want as long as both agree to it, so that a day after the wedding, both husband and wife can hold hands and joyfully journey off to the municipal offices to change their passports, driver's licences, signatures, initials, bank accounts, etc.

## Eighth Suggestion

Teach her to reject likeability. Her job is not to make herself likeable, her job is to be her full self, a self that is honest and aware of the equal humanity of other people. Remember I told you how upsetting it was to me that our friend Chioma would often tell me that 'people' would not 'like' something I wanted to say or do? I always felt, from her, the unspoken pressure to change myself to fit some mould that would please an amorphous entity called 'people'. It was upsetting because we want those close to us to encourage us to be our most authentic selves.

Please do not ever put this pressure on your daughter. We teach girls to be likeable, to be nice, to be false. And we do not teach boys the same. This is dangerous. Many sexual predators have capitalized on this. Many girls remain silent when abused because they want to be nice. Many girls spend too much time trying to be 'nice' to people who do them harm. Many girls think of the 'feelings' of those who are hurting them. This is the catastrophic consequence of likeability. We have a world full of women who are unable to exhale fully because they have for so long been conditioned to fold themselves into shapes to make themselves likeable.

So instead of teaching Chizalum to be likeable, teach her to be honest. And kind.

And brave. Encourage her to speak her mind, to say what she really thinks, to speak truthfully. And then praise her when she does. Praise her especially when she takes a stand that is difficult or unpopular because it happens to be her honest position. Tell her that kindness matters. Praise her when she is kind to other people. But teach her that her kindness must never be taken for granted. Tell her that she too deserves the kindness of others. Teach her to stand up for what is hers. If another child takes her toy without her permission, ask her to take it back, because her consent is important. Tell her that if anything ever makes her uncomfortable, to speak up, to say it, to shout.

Show her that she does not need to be liked by everyone. Tell her that if someone does not like her, there *will* be someone else who will. Teach her that she is not merely an object to be liked or disliked, she is also a subject who can like or dislike. In her teenage years, if she comes home crying about some boys who don't like her, let her know she can choose not to like those boys – yes, it's hard, I know, just remembering my crush on Nnamdi in secondary school.

But still I wish somebody had told me this.

# Ninth Suggestion

Give Chizalum a sense of identity. It matters. Be deliberate about it. Let her grow up to think of herself as, among other things, a proud Igbo woman. And you must be selective – teach her to embrace the parts of Igbo culture that are beautiful and teach her to reject the parts that are not. You can say to her, in different contexts and different ways, 'Igbo culture is lovely because it values community and consensus and hard work, and the language and proverbs are beautiful and full of great wisdom. But Igbo culture also teaches that a woman cannot do certain things just because she's a woman and that is wrong. Igbo culture also focuses a little too much on materialism, and while money is important – because money means self-reliance – you must not value people based on who has money and who does not.'

Be deliberate also about showing her the enduring beauty and resilience of Africans and of black people. Why? Because of the power dynamics in the world, she will grow up seeing images of white beauty, white ability and white achievement, no matter where she is in the world. It will be in the TV shows she watches, in the popular culture she consumes, in the books she reads. She will also probably grow up seeing many negative images of blackness and of Africans.

Teach her to take pride in the history of Africans, and in the black diaspora. Find black heroes, men and women, in history. They exist. You might have to counter some of the things she will learn in school – the Nigerian curriculum isn't quite infused with the idea of teaching children to have a sense of pride in their history. So her teachers will be fantastic at teaching her mathematics and science and art and music, but you will have to do the pride-teaching yourself.

Teach her about privilege and inequality and the importance of giving dignity to everyone who does not mean her harm – teach her

because of the obvious health benefits but because it can help with all the body-image insecurities that the world thrusts on girls. Let Chizalum know that there is great value in being active. Studies show that girls generally stop playing sports as puberty arrives. Not surprising. Breasts and self-consciousness can get in the way of sports – I stopped playing football when my breasts first appeared because all I wanted to do was hide the existence of my breasts, and running and tackling didn't help. Please try not to let that get in her way.

If she likes make-up, let her wear it. If she likes fashion, let her dress up. But if she doesn't like either, let her be. Don't think that raising her feminist means forcing her to reject femininity. Feminism and femininity are not mutually exclusive. It is misogynistic to suggest that they are. Sadly, women have learned to be ashamed and apologetic about pursuits that are seen as traditionally female, such as fashion and make-up. But our society does not expect men to feel ashamed of pursuits considered generally male – sports cars, certain professional sports. In the same way, men's grooming is never suspect in the way women's grooming is – a well-dressed man does not worry that, because he is dressed well, certain assumptions might be made about his intelligence, his ability, or his seriousness. A woman, on the other hand, is always aware of how a bright lipstick or a carefully put-together outfit might very well make others assume her to be frivolous.

Never ever link Chizalum's appearance with morality. Never tell her that a short skirt is 'immoral'. Make dressing a question of taste and attractiveness instead of a question of morality. If you both clash over what she wants to wear, never say things like 'You look like a prostitute', as I know your mother once told you. Instead say: 'That dress doesn't flatter you like this other one.' Or doesn't fit as well. Or doesn't look as attractive. Or is simply ugly. But never 'immoral'. Because clothes have absolutely nothing to do with morality.

Try not to link hair with pain. I think of my childhood and how often I cried while my dense long hair was being plaited. I think of how a packet of Smarties was kept in front of me as a reward if I sat through having my hair done. And for what? Imagine if we had not spent so many Saturdays of our childhood and teenagehood doing our hair. What might we have learned? In what ways might we have grown? What did boys do on Saturdays?

So with her hair, I suggest that you redefine 'neat'. Part of the reason that hair is about pain for so many girls is that adults are determined to conform to a version of 'neat' that means Too Tight and Scalp-Destroying and Headache-Infusing.

We need to stop. I've seen girls in school in Nigeria being terribly harassed for their hair not being 'neat', merely because some of their God-given hair had curled up in glorious tight little balls at their temples. Make Chizalum's hair loose – big plaits and big cornrows, and don't use a tiny-toothed comb that wasn't made with our hair texture in mind.

And make that your definition of neat. Go to her school and talk to the administration if you have to. It takes one person to make change happen.

Chizalum will notice very early on – because children are perceptive – what kind of beauty the mainstream world values. She will see it in magazines and films and television. She will see that whiteness is valued. She will notice that the hair texture that is valued is straight or swingy, and hair that is valued falls down rather than stands up. She will encounter these values whether you like it or not. So make sure that you create alternatives for her to see. Let her know that slim white women are beautiful, and that non-slim, non-white women are beautiful. Let her know that there are many individuals and many cultures that do not find the narrow mainstream definition of beauty attractive. You will know your child best, and so you will know best how to affirm her own kind of beauty, how to protect her from looking at her own reflection with dissatisfaction.

Surround her with a village of aunties, women who have qualities you'd like her to admire. Talk about how much you admire them. Children copy and learn from example. Talk about what you admire about them. I, for example, particularly admire the African American feminist Florynce Kennedy. Some African women that I would tell her about are Ama Ata Aidoo, Dora Akunyili, Muthoni Likimani, Ngozi Okonjo-Iweala, Taiwo Ajai-Lycett. There are so many African women who are sources of feminist inspiration. Because of what they have done and because of what they have refused to do. Like your grandmother, by the way, that remarkable, strong, sharp-tongued babe.

Surround Chizalum, too, with a village of uncles. This will be harder, judging from the kind of friends Chudi has. I still cannot get over that blustering man with the over-carved beard who kept saying at Chudi's last birthday party, 'Any woman I marry cannot tell me what to do!!'

So please find some good non-blustering men. Men like your brother Ugomba, men like our friend Chinakueze. Because the truth is that she will encounter a lot of male bluster in her life. So it is good to have alternatives from very early on.

I cannot overstate the power of alternatives. She can counter ideas about static 'gender roles' if she has been empowered by her familiarity with alternatives. If she knows an uncle who cooks well – and does so with indifference – then she can smile and brush off the foolishness of somebody who claims that 'women must do the cooking'.

# Eleventh Suggestion

Teach her to question our culture's selective use of biology as 'reasons' for social norms.

I know a Yoruba woman, married to an Igbo man, who was pregnant with her first child and was thinking of first names for the child. All the names were Igbo.

Shouldn't her children have Yoruba first names since they would have their father's Igbo surname? I asked, and she said, 'A child first belongs to the father. It has to be that way.'

We often use biology to explain the privileges that men have, the most common reason being men's physical superiority. It is of course true that men are in general physically stronger than women. But if we truly depended on biology as the root of social norms, then children would be identified as their mother's rather than their father's because when a child is born, the parent we are biologically – and incontrovertibly – certain of is the mother. We assume the father is who the mother says the father is. How many lineages all over the world are not biological, I wonder?

For many Igbo women, the conditioning is so complete that women think of children *only* as the father's. I know of women who have left bad marriages but not been 'allowed' to take their children or even to see their children because the children belong to the man.

We also use evolutionary biology to explain male promiscuity, but not to explain female promiscuity, even though it really makes evolutionary sense for women to have many sexual partners – the larger the genetic pool, the greater will be the chances of bearing offspring who will thrive.

So teach Chizalum that biology is an interesting and fascinating subject, but she should never accept it as justification for any social norm. Because social norms are created by human beings, and there is no social norm that cannot be changed.

# Twelfth Suggestion

Talk to her about sex, and start early. It will probably be a bit awkward but it is necessary.

Remember that seminar we went to in class 3 where we were supposed to be taught about 'sexuality' but instead we listened to vague semi-threats about how 'talking to boys' would end up with us being pregnant and disgraced? I remember that hall and that seminar as a place filled with shame. Ugly shame. The particular brand of shame that has to do with being female. May your daughter never encounter it.

With her, don't pretend that sex is merely a controlled act of reproduction. Or an 'only in marriage' act, because that is disingenuous. (You and Chudi were having sex long before marriage and she will probably know this by the time she is twelve.) Tell her that sex can be a beautiful thing and that, apart from the obvious physical consequences (for her as the woman!), it can also have emotional consequences. Tell her that her body belongs to her and her alone, that she should never feel the need to say yes to something she does not want, or something she feels pressured to do. Teach her that saying no when no feels right is something to be proud of.

Tell her you think it's best to wait until she is an adult before she has sex. But be prepared because she might not wait until she's eighteen. And if she doesn't wait, you have to make sure she is able to tell you that she hasn't.

It's not enough to say you want to raise a daughter who can tell you anything; you have to give her the language to talk to you. And I mean this in a literal way. What should she call it? What word should she use?

I remember people used 'ike' when I was a child to mean both 'anus' and 'vagina'; 'anus' was the easier meaning but it left everything vague and I never quite knew how to say, for example, that I had an itch in my vagina.

Most childhood development experts say it is best to have children call sexual organs by their proper biological names – vagina and penis. I agree, but that is a decision you have to make. You should decide what name you want her to call it, but what matters is that there must be a name and that it cannot be a name that is weighed down with shame.

To make sure she doesn't inherit shame from you, you have to free yourself of your own inherited shame. And I know how terribly difficult that is. In every culture in the world, female sexuality is about shame. Even cultures that expect women to be sexy – like many in the West – still do not expect them to be sexual.

The shame we attach to female sexuality is about control. Many cultures and religions control women's bodies in one way or another. If the justification for controlling women's bodies were about women themselves, then it would be understandable. If, for example, the reason was 'women should not wear short skirts because they can get cancer if they do'. Instead the reason is not about women, but about men. Women must be 'covered up' to protect men. I find this deeply dehumanizing because it reduces women to mere props used to manage the appetites of men.

And speaking of shame – never, ever link sexuality and shame. Or nakedness and shame. Do not ever make 'virginity' a focus. Every conversation about virginity becomes a conversation about shame. Teach her to reject the linking of shame and female biology. Why were we raised to speak in low tones about periods? To be filled with shame if our menstrual blood happened to stain our skirt? Periods are nothing to be ashamed of. Periods are normal and natural, and the human species would not be here if periods did not exist. I remember a man who said a period was like shit. Well, sacred shit, I told him, because you wouldn't be here if periods didn't happen.

# Thirteenth Suggestion

Romance will happen, so be on board.

I'm writing this assuming she is heterosexual – she might not be, obviously. But I am assuming that because it is what I feel best equipped to talk about.

Make sure you are aware of the romance in her life. And the only way you can do that is to start very early to give her the language with which to talk to you not only about sex but also about love. I don't mean you should be her 'friend'; I mean you should be her mother to whom she can talk about everything.

Teach her that to love is not only to give but also to take. This is important because we give girls subtle cues about their lives – we teach girls that a large component of their ability to love is their ability to sacrifice their selves. We do not teach this to boys. Teach her that to love she must give of herself emotionally but she must also expect to be given to.

I think love is the most important thing in life. Whatever kind, however you define it, but I think of it generally as being greatly valued by another human being and greatly valuing another human being. But why do we raise only one half of the world to value this? I was recently in a roomful of young women and was struck by how much of the conversation was about men – what terrible things men had done to them, this man cheated, this man lied, this man promised marriage and disappeared, this husband did this and that.

And I realized, sadly, that the reverse is not true. A roomful of men do not invariably end up talking about women – and if they do, it is more likely to be in flippant terms rather than as lamentations of life. Why?

It goes back, I think, to that early conditioning. At a recent baby's baptism ceremony, guests were asked to write their wishes for the baby girl. One guest wrote: 'I wish for you a good husband.' Well-intentioned but very troubling. A three-month-old baby girl already being told that a husband is something to aspire to. Had the baby been a boy, it would not have occurred to that guest to wish for him 'a good wife'.

And speaking of women lamenting about men who 'promise' marriage and then disappear – isn't it odd that in most societies in the world today, women generally cannot propose marriage? Marriage is such a major step in your life and yet you cannot take charge of it; it depends on a man asking you. So many women are in long-term relationships and want to get married but have to wait for the man to propose – and often this waiting becomes a performance, sometimes unconscious and sometimes not, of marriage-worthiness. If we apply the first Feminism Tool here, then it makes no sense that a woman who matters equally has to wait for somebody else to initiate what will be a major life change for her.

A Feminism Lite adherent once told me that the fact that our society expects men to make proposals proves that women have the power, because only if a woman says yes can marriage happen. The truth is this – the real power resides in the person who asks. Before you can say yes or no, you first must be asked. I truly wish for Chizalum a world in which either person can propose, in which a relationship has become so comfortable, so joy-filled, that whether or not to embark on marriage becomes a conversation, itself filled with joy.

I want to say something about money here. Teach her never ever to say such nonsense as 'my money is my money and his money is our money'. It is vile. And dangerous – to have that attitude means that you must potentially accept other harmful ideas as well. Teach her that it is NOT a man's role to provide. In a healthy relationship, it is the role of whoever can provide to provide.

# Fourteenth Suggestion

In teaching her about oppression, be careful not to turn the oppressed into saints. Saintliness is not a prerequisite for dignity. People who are unkind and dishonest are still human, and still deserve dignity. Property rights for rural Nigerian women, for example, is a major feminist issue, and the women do not need to be good and angelic to be allowed their property rights.

There is sometimes, in the discourse around gender, the assumption that women are supposed to be morally 'better' than men. They are not. Women are as human as men are. Female goodness is as normal as female evil.

And there are many women in the world who do not like other women. Female misogyny exists, and to evade acknowledging it is to create unnecessary opportunities for anti-feminists to try to discredit feminism. I mean the sort of anti-feminists who will gleefully raise examples of women saying 'I am not a feminist' as though a person born with a vagina making this statement somehow automatically discredits feminism. That a woman claims not to be feminist does not diminish the necessity of feminism. If anything, it makes us see the extent of the problem, the successful reach of patriarchy. It shows us, too, that not all women are feminists and not all men are misogynists.

# Fifteenth Suggestion

Teach her about difference. Make difference ordinary. Make difference normal. Teach her not to attach value to difference. And the reason for this is not to be fair or to be nice but merely to be human and practical. Because difference is the reality of our world. And by teaching her about difference, you are equipping her to survive in a diverse world.

She must know and understand that people walk different paths in the world and that as long as those paths do no harm to others, they are valid paths that she must respect. Teach her that we do not know – we cannot know – everything about life. Both religion and science have spaces for the things we do not know, and it is enough to make peace with that.

Teach her never to universalize her own standards or experiences. Teach her that her standards are for her alone, and not for other people. This is the only necessary form of humility: the realization that difference is normal.

Tell her that some people are gay, and some are not. A little child has two daddies or two mummies because some people just do. Tell her that some people go to mosque and others go to church and others go to different places of worship and still others don't worship at all, because that is just the way it is for some people.

You say to her: You like palm oil but some people don't like palm oil.

She says to you: Why?

You say to her: I don't know. It's just the way the world is.

Please note that I am not suggesting that you raise her to be 'non-judgemental', which is a commonly used expression these days, and which slightly worries me. The general sentiment behind the idea is a fine one, but 'non-judgemental' can easily devolve into meaning 'don't have an opinion about anything' or 'I keep my opinions to myself'. And so, instead of that, what I hope for Chizalum is this: that she will be full of opinions, and that her opinions will come from an informed, humane and broad-minded place.

May she be healthy and happy. May her life be whatever she wants it to be.

Do you have a headache after reading all this? Sorry. Next time don't ask me how to raise your daughter feminist.

With love, oyi gi,
Chimamanda

# About the Author

Chimamanda Ngozi Adichie grew up in Nigeria. Her work has been translated into thirty languages and has appeared in various publications, including *The New Yorker*, *Granta*, *The O. Henry Prize Stories*, the *Financial Times* and *Zoetrope: All-Story*. She is the author of the novels *Purple Hibiscus*, which won the Commonwealth Writers' Prize and the Hurston/Wright Legacy Award; *Half of a Yellow Sun*, which won the Orange Prize and was a National Book Critics Circle Award finalist, a *New York Times* Notable Book, and a *People* and *Black Issues Book Review* Best Book of the Year; *Americanah*, which won the

National Book Critics Circle Award and was a *New York Times*, *Washington Post*, *Chicago Tribune* and *Entertainment Weekly* Best Book of the Year; the story collection *The Thing Around Your Neck*; and the essay *We Should All Be Feminists*. A recipient of a MacArthur Fellowship, she divides her time between the United States and Nigeria.

www.chimamanda.com
www.facebook.com/chimamandaadichie